The Surrender Project

A personal journey… learning how to slow down, trust and find power in your softness as you harness your innate feminine wisdom.

LAUREN KERR

BALBOA.PRESS
A DIVISION OF HAY HOUSE

Balboa Press books may be ordered through booksellers or by contacting:

Balboa Press
A Division of Hay House
1663 Liberty Drive
Bloomington, IN 47403
www.balboapress.com.au
AU TFN: 1 800 844 925 (Toll Free inside Australia)
AU Local: (02) 8310 7086 (+61 2 8310 7086 from outside Australia)

Print information available on the last page.

ISBN: 978-1-9822-9624-7 (sc)
ISBN: 978-1-9822-9664-3 (e)

Balboa Press rev. date: 02/13/2023

They always say that to make your first six figures, you have to hustle, but to make your first seven figures, you just change your lifestyle, which is easier said than done when you're used to making moves, running a million miles per hour, and finding your identity and self-worth in your work ethic.

Lauren's first book, *Life Above Zero: Making Mindset Manageable, Health Holistic, Spirituality Science, and Life Liberating,* helps people be in control of their mindset to create a life, a business, and a career that brings them fulfilment.

The Surrender Project is for successful women in the corporate world or entrepreneurs who are faced with the challenge of slowing down and enjoying their success, leaning into their femininity, and preparing for the mental shifts that come with motherhood—a rite of passage that seems to change with each generation with the exceeding demands on women.

Think of it like 'Sex and the City' mixed with 'Eat Pray Love'. An uncensored, personal journey talking about things a lot of women in the 21st century are thinking... but are too scared to say out loud.

Contents

Acknowledgements

We are who we are because of the books we read, the music we listen to, the conversations we have, and the company we keep.

So this book, this project, this journey is a reflection of some amazing people I have in my life, and I want to thank them.

Mum, your voids became my biggest values. Because of you and your honest and raw conversations with me about what it means to be a wife, mum, and woman in your generation … well, look at how many lives we have been able to impact in such a positive way. I'm in awe of the circle of life. As I birth life of my own, only now can I really start to comprehend the sacrifices you made for me and my brothers. I hope I can guide my baby girl in this world as well as you guided your children. I'm so grateful I got to choose you as my mum. It's your love and our relationship that have inspired me to want to be a mum myself. I hope I can be at least half the woman you are to me.

Dad, thanks for making me strong and yet always being a safe haven for me to retreat into—my softness. Thanks for showing me what love is and helping me attract my king, instilling self-worth and belief that I should never settle for anything less.

My king, Sebastian (Dan), thanks for always loving me and supporting me no matter where I have been on my Surrender Project and self-discovery journey. You have shown me nothing but unconditional love, zero judgement, and commitment to grow together. I love you. You are going to be the best dad. Our princess doesn't know how lucky she is that she gets you as her king too.

My soul sister and business bestie, Chani, your softness and patience have been the yin to my yang over the last six years. Your moon wisdom has helped me tap into my faith and femininity. Thank you for constantly, lovingly mirroring back to me parts of myself that were keeping me restricted. We built a business together, and now we are building families. I don't think it's a coincidence that our babies are due on the same exact day! These souls are definitely here to teach us something.

My mentors over the years, Sue (from Child Safety), Kate, Linda, Loren, Cheryl, and Celine in the Juice Plus Company, I have been so fortunate to have been surrounded with mentors and women I want to emulate—women who are breaking a lot of the stereotypes I was brought up with and thought I had to expect and accept in life as a mother, a wife, career woman, and creator of wealth. I am surrounded by women who are examples of having it all without sacrifice—which I didn't know was an option for me. You have shown me a way to have financial independence but also a loving marriage. You have shown the power of leading with femininity and softness instead of demanding authority with masculinity. And you have shown a way I can be a present, loving stay-at-home mum whilst also being a CEO of an international multimillion-dollar business who earns an abundant income. Before Juice Plus, I didn't know there was a way I could choose this *and* that. I thought (as I had seen from the lineage of women before me) that I could have this, *but it would be at expense* of that.

My team and the amazing women I get to work with online, you are New Age women who are rewriting history and redefining how life is meant to be. You are creating new narratives for our daughters and for our ancestors who fought hard for the freedom and choices we have today. Every day you inspire me because you break biases. You don't just talk about what women are capable of; you show them. You are amazing mums, wives, employees, bosses, leaders, and friends. And you do it all whilst also showing other women how you can create a smart second income through collaboration and caring, not competition. I know you defy a lot of society's expectations—going to school, getting a degree, being a good girl, staying in line as you make your way up a corporate ladder or stay at home to raise the kids. You go against the grain (which a lot of the time initially comes at the expense of loved ones' support) to prove to other ambitious women that it can be done. You are openminded women who can have it all (and don't have it do it alone). Success is available to everyone; sometimes people just need to see other brave women going first. So, my team, thank you for going first and holding open a space in which I can grow as a person, as a woman, and as a leader.

My spirit guides, I used to think I was crazy; now I know I'm not. I was crazy to think I had to do life alone. Life is so much more fun and magical since I have welcomed you into it, and it flows with more ease.

There are many who will never know how much they have impacted my life and helped me lean into my femininity and be softer in my leadership and marriage. Mentors don't also have to be people in your orbit!

> Kristen Jenna. For guiding me through my spiritual awakening without even knowing it. Thanks for going first.

> Gabby Bernstein, author of *The Universe Has Your Back: Transform Fear to Faith* and *Super Attractor: Methods for Manifesting a Life beyond Your Wildest Dreams*

> Wednesday Martin, author of *Untrue: Why Nearly Everything We Believe About Women, Lust, and Infidelity Is Wrong and How the New Science Can Set Us Free*

Christopher Ryan, author of *Sex at Dawn: How We Mate, Why We Stray, and What It Means* by Cacilda Jethá

Kate Northrup, author of *Do Less: A Revolutionary Approach to Time and Energy Management for Ambitious Women*

Gina Devee, author of *The Audacity to be Queen: The Unapologetic Art of Dreaming Big and Manifesting Your Most Fabulous Life*

Eckhart Tolle, author of *A New Earth: Awakening to Your Life's Purpose*

Alison Armstrong, author of *Keys to the Kingdom*

Alisa Vitti, author of *In the FLO: Unlock Your Hormonal Advantage and Revolutionize Your Life*

Rebecca Campbell, author of *Light Is the New Black: A Guide to Answering Your Soul's Callings and Working Your Light*

Emma Mildon, author of *Evolution of Goddess: A Modern Girl's Guide to Activating Your Feminine Superpowers*

Yamile Yemoonyah, author of *The Seven Types of Spirit Guide*

Sex and City television series—the OG empowered woman pick me up! Even when I was a little girl, this series had a big influence on me and taught me the power of sisterhood. It helped me realise the need for women to have honest and raw conversations. It helped me realise that we have rights and the ability to question the status quo and what we expect and accept in our careers and relationships.

Chani Thompson's Moon Magic Master class and the Cycle Syncing Masterclass on The Healthstyle Emporium website.

And lastly, to you, beautiful woman. Thanks for coming along for the wild ride. I hope *The Surrender Project* will challenge your beliefs, support you through the discomfort of growth, and guide you to soften into your faith and femininity too.

We aren't crazy. We are wild! Our ancient women's wisdom is written in the moon and stars. We aren't meant to be tamed or restrained.

Keep surrendering.

The Prelude

I am so excited (and to be honest a tad nervous) to share with you a personal project I've been working on over the last two years. It is *The Surrender Project*—the diaries of a recovering "human doing."

In this uncensored, personal, two-year journey, I talk about topics I think a lot of us women in the twenty-first century are thinking but are too scared to say out loud. It's real and raw. I talk about drugs, sex, and rock and roll (if Kings of Leon and Fleetwood Mac count?). This comes from the inner workings of my crazy mind.

Think of it kinda like *Sex and the City* mixed with *Eat Pray Love*, all in the format of a series of diary entries.

When I started, I didn't know where we would end up, but that's the point, right? Surrendering control.

Come along for the journey if you would love to see if what I have learned in my personal project could help you slow down too and start being a "human being" instead of a "human (constantly) doing."

Anything goes. The only rule is that I let my husband preview each chapter. Because, although I'm happy to bare all, that doesn't mean he is too.

I always tell my coaching clients and women I mentor in business that the magic happens out of your comfort zone. If you're scared—good.

Lean in. It means you're growing. You're evolving. Something exciting is about to happen.

I have occasionally been scared to share these words on paper. Scared of being vulnerable. Scared of judgement.

But I am walking my talk, trusting my intuition, and taking inspired action (even when it feels scary).

Come join me for my own personal Surrender Project, from start to end, and witness my beliefs and reality evolve.

Be warned: considering these are "diary entries," they are probably what a lot of women are thinking but not saying out loud.

Unlike my first book, *Life Above Zero*, which reflects a lot of education, research, and psychology, this book is more personal. It is written in a conversational tone, and as I start to explore my own spirituality, I delve into areas that research can't always explain and our brains can't rationalise or see. This is different from my usual content and what you may be used to from me. It is just a little more intimate, juicy, and probably more controversial.

These are my uncensored diary entries. Not the facts. Not the truth. Just the way I (sometimes struggle to) see the world through my tainted goggles.

I am not here to change your mind or argue with you about certain subjects I am personally navigating. I am just having arguments with my own inner critic (she is a crazy bitch) and airing out my own dirty laundry and baggage so other women and fellow human doings out there can have a laugh and realise they aren't alone in their own f#*ked-up thoughts.

So, if you're still here, it must mean you are a little wild and crazy too.

I like you.

See you on the other side, beautiful.

Diary Entry 1

Relinquish control. Surrender to faith. Allow joy

HI, I AM LAUREN. AND I AM A RECOVERING *HUMAN DOING.*

It's May 2020. It's been an interesting year, globally and personally. In Australia, we started the year with horrific bushfires and are currently navigating a global pandemic as I write this, which has propelled the world into a financial crisis and a standstill. The whole world has stopped. There is such a strange energy in the air—uncertainty yet rejuvenation.

I have spent the last six years hustling to finish my psychology degree. It feels as if I even spent the years up to that hustling, juggling sports, high school, a social life, boyfriend, and employment.

I worked hard to get into university. I worked hard to get high distinctions to get into honours courses. I worked hard to get a graduate position. I worked hard to study life coaching and create a side hustle around my nine-to-six workday (and two-hour commute). I worked hard to make my side hustle replace my full-time income in eighteen months and hit the top position in my company. And, for the last few years, I have felt as if I have been working hard to duplicate that and keep that momentum going.

Don't get me wrong; it's not as if it's been a hard slog or as if I've gone without. The majority of this journey has felt in flow and alignment as I took inspired action towards things my heart desired and soul yearned for. There have been lots of magical moments with friends and family members. There has been personal, professional, and spiritual growth. And there have been accolades, travel, and money to invest back into myself. All of this has made my efforts worthwhile and fuelled me for the next goal.

But it's as if I have hit a wall.

There is no gas left in the tank.

I wonder if this is what people refer to as burnout?

I am regularly told I am a unicorn, but I always just figured that this is what you have got to do if you want to be successful. I am not a unicorn. I am just a realist. I have a get-shit-done attitude. I know that, if I want something, I have got to go out there and get it or do it for myself.

It's not for recognition, accolades, or attention. It's pretty selfish I guess. It's for me. It's for the lifestyle I want to create, the moments I want to experience, and the profession I want to enjoy. It's my character. That work and those actions are what I would do regardless of whether anyone was watching or patting my back.

It's my identity. Which, I guess, is why this chapter of life feels so uncomfortable for me.

Slowing down.

I find my flow in pursuing goals, taking action, and being productive—getting shit done. But every fibre in my body is resistant to that at this very moment.

I just finished writing my book *Life Above Zero* last year. I feel as if it took three years of hustling to bring that bad boy to life. The writing itself was easy, in flow. I enjoyed lots of inspired action. But after it was written and edited, and after I finally secured a contract with a publisher (after lots of rejections), it was met with roadblock after roadblock.

I felt that, after I got all the words on paper, every scrap of inspiration left my body. I had nothing left to say, no purpose, nothing tugging at me to pursue.

So I just waited and listened. I waited for my intuition to come back.

The coronavirus pandemic pushed back the anticipated book launch because my books were stuck overseas, bookstores had closed, and my flights to Melbourne to record the audio version in a studio were cancelled.

I felt uninspired with my business. The thought of hustling or pushing made me want to self-destruct and blow it all up.

I know enough by now through studying psychology and being in business with and mentoring thousands of other women over the last four years to know that I was about to embark on my next level.

The resistance was forcing me to sit in discomfort and look within.

Something I was already aware of and working on was my belief in the idea that I needed to work hard to create abundance. Don't get me wrong, I believe in business—it does take a few years of hustle to get that beast off the ground and profitable. However, if you have to rely purely on your effort and hustle to continue to grow and scale your business, you don't have a business; you have a glorified job.

I knew this theoretically. But I was really working on conceptualising and applying it.

This year I invested in a business and marketing coach to help me get out of the six-figure hamster wheel and create more white space in my day to stop *doing* and start *being*.

Being the typical human doing, I did everything he told me to.

To be honest I've tried not to be jealous of all the people using the new pandemic way of life to slow down and sit on their asses, because I have been working my little ass off.

Here's what I've done in the last ninety days:

3

- I invested in myself and spent a month's worth of income on a business and marketing coach.
- I completed an intensive marketing program to level up my skills.
- I finally got around to filming and creating my six-month life and mindset coaching program.
- I wrote nearly six months' worth of copy and content.
- I hired a team and finally outsourced everything in my business that doesn't bring me joy.
- I signed a contract with a publisher for the audio rights to my book.
- I welcomed and mentored twenty-five new women in business to create an income from home.
- I finally got around to recording my book in a recording studio (the publisher found one here on the Gold Coast considering we can't fly at the moment).
- We wrote a thirty-five-page side hustle e-guide that we gift for free on our Babes Talking Business website (https://babesinbusiness.net/) to educate women about money. (I am really proud of this.)
- I worked with a website developer and created my very own free thirty-minute online quiz to help people find their happiness.
- I continued to manage my usual workload with my existing online business, support my clients, and record episodes for our podcast.

I share this to not impress you (or maybe that recovering human doing in me is looking for a pat on the back after all), but because I hate it when people compare themselves to other people's highlight reels on social media.

You can always trust me to be real with you, so I wanted to share with you what you don't see behind the scenes. I do this to reassure any other ambitious women out there who might be wondering if anyone else is working as hard as they are to make their dreams come true—I am.

You may not see me posting about it (because I'm busy actually doing it), but this won't last forever. It can't. My soul, body, and business—physically, spiritually, and logically—won't allow it to.

So here I am, sitting in the discomfort, facing the resistance and trying to listen. Is it time to pivot? Is there no more gas in the tank because I have taken this path as far as it can go? Am I just being lazy?

This is the very thing that grinds my gears, and it is what I condemn in others—sitting around and doing nothing isn't going to change anything.

Do I just need to get off my ass and make shit happen? Am I too comfortable?

I now have everything I once wanted—those things that used to drive me. Is it time to just dig deeper and find a new "why" to get hungry again? Despite slowing down, is this me actively working on overcoming self-limiting beliefs so I can transcend to the next level of abundance?

Is this just my next devil for the level of business I am in to help me break down the belief that I need to work hard to make money and instead learning to trust and experience residual income I have worked so hard to create?

Or am I just looking into it all too much, and my adrenals are simply just telling me it's time to rest?

Whatever the answers to these questions are, I know I have to listen because I have no choice. There is no *umph*. There is an energetic block, and I am being forced to be still.

I know my mum will be happy. For over a decade now she has been telling me to slow down and smell the flowers.

So, thanks for coming to my recovery meeting.

I am Lauren, and I am a recovering human doing.

I am assuming that, because you are here, you're a recovering human doing too.

Well, I'm proclaiming that I'm coming into my season of flow—my season of rest, rejuvenation, restoration, and reflection. My season of being.

I have no idea where this is going to lead me, but my mantra for the next few months is "follow what feels good."

I can hear my intuition again quietly encouraging me to write, so I am listening.

This is my Surrender Project.

Diary Entry 2

An anxiety attack

HERE SHE COMES. I'VE BEEN EXPECTING HER.

I thought I had caught onto her sneaky plan before she arrived. I've got good at picking up her cues and trying to catch her before she rudely overtakes my control—uninvited may I add.

Nevertheless, I feel anxiety this afternoon. My breathing is shallow. I feel butterflies, and my heart is racing fast (as if I have drunk three espresso martinis). I have that hollow feeling in the pit of my stomach as if I am thirteen again and am about to get caught by my parents and get in trouble for what I got up to on the weekend.

But this time I have done nothing wrong.

I am a full-grown adult. (If I can honestly claim that. Do we ever actually grow up?) I haven't even left the house today to get into any mischief. My brain is manic, and my mean girl is up to her old tricks again; she's taunting me.

She makes no sense. Her thoughts dart around following no logical order and adding nothing constructive or positive to the discussion.

It's okay though.

Over the last ten years, I have got pretty good at ignoring her and learning how to drown her out through exercise, nourishing foods, meditation, education, and compassion.

So, in my attempt to kindly ask her to leave so I can regain control of my breath and head space, I have run myself a warm bath, thrown in a bath bomb, and lit a yummy candle so I can retreat into a warm, lavender-scented sea whilst listening to an audio book I have been enjoying, one that actually has something positive to say and is worth listening to.

She doesn't like that.

She gets louder and demands her presence to be felt. I feel her expanding and taking up all the space within me as she makes her way up from my belly to my heart to my chest to my throat, squeezing out the little breath and control I have left.

She forces me to get out of the bath and lie on the cold tiles, naked and in silence. To do nothing but be still and present and to focus on nothing but my breath.

Time stands still. With my undivided attention and focus, her waves calm as quickly as they stormed in. And, oddly, I am left feeling very peaceful and connected.

Something encouraged me to grab a diary and start writing because my intuition had something to say. So I did. And a download came through.

Now, before I share with you the rest, I feel the need to explain that I am not a complete fruit loop (or maybe I am?). I am pretty rational and logical. I am a realist who believes in and relies on science and evidence. If you have read my previous book, *Life Above Zero*, you know and understand this.

But another thing I do believe in (yet do not truly understand) is spirituality. But I guess that is the point, isn't it? Faith is not so much about seeing; it is believing in something you cannot see, explain, or rationalise.

I have always had faith and believed in the power we hold in our beliefs rather than our ability, which is why I have *faith* tattooed on my wrist, the reason I studied psychology, and also why I was inspired to write my previous book to share the research findings around that for other rational people out there struggling to find meaning and have faith.

I'm still exploring what spirituality means to me personally.

I have learned to trust and believe in the universal laws. Over the last ten years, I have witnessed my own intuition, and I have built confidence in my intuitive feelings. In *Life Above Zero*, I describe it as that tug in the gut. It's your own moral compass. Your soul uses it to navigate this crazy life and help you find the path that aligns most with your highest desires, to do the highest good, and enable you to fulfil your soul's work and live on purpose, in purpose.

My intuition went walkabout after I finished writing *Life Above Zero* over a year ago. She left me with only my logical brain, who is kind of boring. My logical brain doesn't see all the magic and infinite possibilities; neither does it believe in miracles

To be honest, my life felt pretty dull and monotonous after my intuition left. With the pandemic constraining me within four walls, all travel plans (including our honeymoon) being cancelled for the year, I was left with no muse. No inspiration. Just me. Sitting with my discomfort.

So, when this download from my intuition came through, I recognised it as my intuition returning! And I have learned to trust her, so I started scribing as it flowed:

Okay, It's time to listen.

Anxiety isn't anxiety. It's a download. It's connection.
It's me prompting you to sit in quiet to connect and lean

into me. I've been trying to connect with you for a long time, but I understand now that you're ready.

The book *Super Attractor: Methods for Manifesting a Life beyond Your Wildest Dreams* by Gabrielle Bernstein is your angel guiding you. She's trying to help you connect with me. I'm an archangel. You've been pulling my cards; go see who I am.

But first, here is what I have to tell you:

Stop doing. Surrender. Relinquish control. Surrender to faith. Allow joy. Stop doing!

Just connect, follow the signs and, when you can't hear me, just choose joy and do what feels good.

No more doing, no more new projects besides writing. This might be a book and your opportunity to make spirituality science, but this is your spiritual journey.

That word *faith* tattooed on your wrist is a seed you planted many years ago, and now you're about to start walking down the path.

No more personal development. No more consuming. Just creating.

Ace was looking at me when you picked him up this week.

I made you choose the blue bath bomb.

And I made sure the Surrender Project was sent to you.

I made sure that you finished doing your business projects before connecting back with yourself. Now you need to let go and let abundance flow in. You're needed elsewhere.

When you were young, you felt very in tune. You felt magical. You were connected. You thought you were a fairy. It's time to believe in magic again.

Keep choosing what feels good.

Give up your timeline. I've got you.

Surrender.

I could have cried. I think I did. It was an overwhelming feeling of love, support, disbelief, and trust. I finally felt connected again.

Here is some background for you:

I did get *faith* tattooed on my wrist many years ago. Ten to be exact. It was my eighteenth birthday, and to be honest, I wasn't sure what that word meant to me, but since the age of sixteen, I had written that word on my wrist in the same place every day with a pen, and I figured a tattoo was safer than ink poisoning.

One of my girlfriends just had her first baby, Ace. I met him for the first time last week, and we watched him, curious, as he giggled and smiled as he looked at something above my head. All we could see was a white wall.

I googled what "blue" means spiritually because I was unsure about the reference to the blue bath bomb. I had been shopping the day before and decided to treat myself to a bath bomb from Lush, and I chose one I had never tried before.

The meaning of the colour blue: Blue represents both the sky and the sea and is associated with open spaces, freedom, intuition, imagination, expansiveness, inspiration, and sensitivity. Blue also represents depth, trust, loyalty, sincerity, wisdom, confidence, stability, faith, heaven, and intelligence.

I honoured the instruction to pull a card from my angel tarot deck. I pulled the battle card by the angel Samuel.

> These stories represent the hero standing in the face of danger ready to confront his or her shadow. They represent the hero's willingness to surrender to a higher state of consciousness at the expense of all ego and attachment such as pride, greed, and compulsion.
>
> So as a hero goes out to battle dragons in order to bring the goods back to his own town, he or she is actually going on a journey to face the shadow in order to bring the goods back to himself or herself so that movement can be made into the next phase of life on an internal level.
>
> It may now be time for you to go on this journey.
>
> This is a call to adventure. What are you going to fight for? This is a call to arms!

I have no idea what it all meant, but I have made myself a promise to surrender and always trust the flow and the tug in my gut.

I feel things shifting, and I am leaning in.

Diary Entry 3

Testing it out

OKAY, LET'S TRY THIS SURRENDER PROJECT OUT.

I am consciously slowing down, leaning into what feels good, honouring saying no to new projects, and trying to be more present.

This is what has transpired:

This week I signed up my first client to the mindset and life coaching program that I have been working on. She found me via a guest podcast I had been on. There had been no relationship building beforehand. I built my business through relationship building during the previous four years, spending three to four hours a day in my inbox growing my network and investing and building relationships.

She had booked a call directly via my website. It was easy. No pushing. No selling. No objection management. Just pure exchange of energy.

I shared my gifts and what I enjoy, my zone of genius.

She appreciated that, enjoyed that, and wanted more, so she paid up front for her coaching and mindset program.

I know that, when it comes to changing beliefs, we need to look for evidence to support the contrary. I'm not sure if I could claim I am a converted believer yet, but I was going to add this incident to my pile of evidence that proves that business can be fun. Money can be abundant and flow with ease when we're aligned with our soul work.

In my last book, I wrote about happiness being habitual. The more happiness we experience, the more we need to get to attain the same level of satisfaction or fulfilment. Well, it's the same with money.

Over the last four years, I have been working so much on myself, my business, and my growth that my income has also simultaneously grown.

You know what they say: your net worth is a direct reflection of your self-worth. But in saying that, I also know that gratitude is the magnet for miracles and for attracting more abundance.

Now, by investing three hours of my time in private coaching (doing something I actually enjoy that I would do for free anyway) I can earn the same amount of money that, once upon a time (four years ago actually, which shows how quickly you can change your life and circumstances), took me an entire month to earn (after tax): 140 hours of my time.

Now if that isn't evidence of flow, I don't know what is!

You hear that, rational brain? I hope you are letting that soak in, you negative nelly who doubts everything and tries to keep me confined within the walls of your limiting beliefs! I will prove you wrong. I am pledged to this Surrender Project and excited to see where it takes us. I am hoping to go places and have experiences that you can't rationalise so you too will choose to let go and trust more.

My younger brother rang me and told me that he and his girlfriend had spontaneously decided that they were going to drive home next week to surprise my mum.

Because of the worldwide pandemic, all flights have been cancelled. Our parents were actually supposed to be on the Gold Coast where I live this week, but with the Queensland borders closed their holiday has been cancelled. Mum has been really sick and bedridden for three weeks. My brother has lost his job in the financial crises. His university has been forced online, so he figured he would make the most of the opportunity and start the sixteen-hour drive on the weekend.

I haven't done that drive since I moved to the Gold Coast ten years ago. We usually fly. It only takes a few hours instead of sixteen. I hate being in a car. I get car sick. I am not a very confident driver. As much as I would love to have gone, it was only a week away. I hadn't planned, it and … and …

There is no *and*. Why was I putting up a wall and making excuses preventing myself from allowing joy?

I put my hand on my heart and asked myself: What would feel good? What would bring me joy?

A week slowing down at home, spending quality time with my family sounded perfect. Family is my highest value and my biggest source of joy. Plus, just seeing the look on mum and dad's faces when we surprise them and pull this off would be priceless.

I reminded myself: Relinquish control, surrender to faith, and allow joy. Relinquish your plans and your timeline, Lauren. Surrender and have faith that this came up because family is exactly where you are meant to be this week.

And it felt good.

Things don't have to be productive or for an intention or purpose other than pure joy, I told myself. Plus, I could sleep in the car, eat lollies, listen to my fav podcast, and use the journey as an opportunity to belt out some old tunes with my not-so-little brother.

Okay, done.

My rational brain didn't need too much convincing.

My publisher had organised and booked me into the recording studio that week to record the audio version of *Life Above Zero* because they couldn't fly me down to Melbourne to record in their studio.

This all worked out perfectly. I needed about five four-hour days in the studio.

The recording project turned out to be experience in itself. I never realised there were so many words I don't pronounce correctly, and recording is more exhausting than you would think. I had to talk four hours straight without sounding like a croaky, husky man. I felt vulnerable sharing my inner workings out loud with someone on the other side of the screen. I knew people were reading the book, I guess reading it out loud just felt different—more raw. It felt as if I was stripped naked and standing right next to someone as I revealed all. And he wasn't even gentleman enough to look away and allow me some privacy as I undressed all my emotional layers with each chapter.

Rude! Or maybe he was just doing his job.

We ended up finishing the recording a day early, so my brother and I got into the car and started the drive home. I felt as if I was seventeen again without a care in the world, being spontaneous and going on a road trip with really nowhere to be by any certain time. The 90s and 2000s playlists blasted through the car speakers whilst I scoffed down a bag of sour worm lollies, probably assisted with the mental trip down memory lane.

The look on mum and dad's faces was priceless. We videoed it to add to our collection so we could replay it over and over again. Over the years, we have pulled off a few surprises, but this one was probably the best. By the look of relief on mum's face, I could tell she really needed some extra love. It felt nice to be able to do that and be that source of joy and comfort for her.

It was a slow week—a pace I wasn't really familiar or comfortable with. But I was considering this my first test.

It sounds pretty funny, doesn't it? Being challenged by slowing down? Like what's the challenge Lauren? Pour yourself a wine, hang out with your family, and chill the f#*k out!

But that's the point. As a human doing, I need to be doing—doing, achieving, pursuing goals, making moves, ticking checklists.

No shit! To try to give my logical brain some kind of comfort, I literally wrote "Me time" in my diary this week so at least I could tick it off as if it was something I had to do.

Pretty messed up, right?

I tried to sit with my thoughts and unpack them. Is it because I find joy in working and doing? Sometimes. But I would rather get paid to sit on my ass in the sunshine with a book and a cocktail.

What? This is my Surrender Project, so I can be honest, right?

I was trying to tease out if it was a self-limiting belief or scarcity mindset. If I stopped working or hustling, would the success, momentum, and money I had created stop? Because, once again, if I am honest, I have to say that I could get paid to sit on my ass.

I have spent the last four years creating a network marketing business that pays me six figures a year in "residual" income. That means that, whether I work today or not, that money still flows into my bank account.

So why wouldn't I just allow it to?

I don't know. I don't have all the answers, and I am not ready to go full cold turkey yet.

This was my week for just testing and feeling it out. And despite the discomfort, it did feel nice.

I still worked a few hours a day, but I got to catch up with my best friend, who also lives in my hometown with her husband. We shared dinners, walks, and random shopping sprees. I didn't feel guilty for enjoying some cocktails in the middle of the week. Who am I to refuse anyway? She makes the best amaretto sours, and her hubby makes the best Mexican! Man, I love those two!

I played board games in the middle of the day with my mum or my brother and sat down to watch Netflix in the afternoons with the family despite having my logical brain taunting me and telling me I was being "naughty" and trying to make me feel guilty.

Guilty for what?

What was I doing that was naughty? What the actual f#★k!

Is it my own messed-up belief system that has conditioned me to think I need to deserve or earn time to slow down? Or is it today's societal expectations that we need to be on the go all the time until we drop dead of a heart attack?

I find myself sometimes being jealous of the native and traditional owners of our land whose "work" once upon a time was just living life—hunting, growing food, preparing meals, teaching their children, building their homes. They have time for joy, connection, family, the outdoors, exercise, and hobbies sprinkled throughout their days.

Today, however, most people carve out eight to ten hours a day and fill it with work that is separate from and at the expense of activities that bring them joy and happiness.

I read that, in the United States, workers take only an average of 50 per cent of their paid vacation days. That's crazy! You've got 90,000 hours to spend for free! Take the chance to chill on the beach when someone gives it to you, or just stay at home and relax, spend time with your family members and friends, enjoy hobbies or do sweet f#★k all with no obligation!

It's even sadder in Japan, where 10,000 workers per year drop dead at their desks as a result of sixty- to seventy-hour work weeks. The phenomenon is so prevalent that it even has a name: *karoshi*.

I know I had personally worked hard (there is that term again: *worked hard*) to get away from that model of working and trading time for money. But it was becoming evident that the residue of that way of thinking was still wedged in the way I thought about business and how I "had to" live and whether I deserved to enjoy my life.

The week came to an end, and I felt as if I had passed my first test with flying colours!

I had sixteen hours on the drive home to mull over it and fill out my scorecard. (As a typical human doer and overachiever, I'm always assessing myself.)

I let the music play as I drove and my brother and his girlfriend slept, and as I drove, the reflections flowed.

Such a weird feeling. I had shed a tear earlier that week trying to label it and explain it to my mum because no one really talks about it or warns us. It's not sadness, and it's not even nostalgia. It's more like a shock to the system as we discover the fragility of permanence.

I moved away from home ten years ago this year. I was freshly eighteen with a life full of vibrant, deep, meaningful, energising, exciting friendships and memories. Every street reminded me of laughter, fun, best mates, summers in love, and drunken nights roaming from one party to another.

But as each year passes, friends move away, people grow older and apart, grandparents pass. Piece by piece, the things that made our hometowns so comforting and familiar fade as we start to build lives for ourselves block by block sixteen hours away.

As I drove around the streets of what once had been my whole world, everything felt void and dull. I realised that the emotions and memories I was looking for I no longer felt or recognised there.

During our visit, we went through old photo albums full of pictures of my parents when they were my age, and then when my brothers and I were babies. I was reminded of my friends who are now starting to have families of their own.

It's crazy watching the circle of life unfold. I am in awe of it and frightened of it at the same time because I realise how quickly time goes by and things change.

I still don't really know how to label it, but I do know that I have amazing friendships and family relationships that make my heart burst with so much gratitude, love, and joy. No matter how much time or distance separates us, tears fill my eyes when I reminisce about all the memories. I want to soak every bit of this life in because things evolve so quickly.

I am so glad I leaned in and listened to my intuition this week when it encouraged me to go home. It felt good.

But after a sixteen-hour-long drive, it's good to be home. The Gold Coast is my comfort now. I just miss my mum and dad.

Diary Entry 4

Sex and a Puppy

So, WHAT FEELS GOOD?

That is the question I keep coming back to in order to ground myself. The idea helps me get clarity and lean into and trust my next step.

I have always wanted a little French bulldog or a pug—a little fawn fatty Pumbaa. I think that's because, when I was growing up, all our family dogs had been that colour, so that conditioned a feeling of familiarity and unconditional love for me.

We had Syd (short for Sydney, named after the Australian Football League team Sydney Swans). He was a boxer crossed with a Rottweiler. JB (short for jellybean) is our fifteen-year-old, now blind and deaf pug who still lives with my parents.

The timing for me getting a dog just hasn't felt right. Because my business and travel are high value for both my husband and I (and because his family live in the UK), we enjoy being able to travel overseas a few times each year, so it really isn't fair to have a little dog in our lives, especially cooped up in our apartment.

Over the last two years, though, I have definitely felt something shift within me. Something longing for a slower pace. A bigger home. More routine and stability. A family.

I am not sure if there is something that clicks in us women at a certain age, but my maternal instinct has been getting stronger. I don't know if I am ready for kids just yet. (I have heard other women say we really never are ready.) But I am ready to settle and start building a home.

Is this what they refer to as nesting?

When my husband and I got married last year, I even put in my wedding vows that I couldn't wait until Dan would allow me to have babies and a Frenchie of our own. I was craving that, but I also knew we weren't in the chapter of our lives—or businesses—where that felt in alignment just yet.

That was before 2020! The year the world came to a standstill.

I am sure everyone's plans got cancelled this year, including ours. It feels as if the entire year was cancelled. We had already booked Bali (twice), London, the Amalfi Coast (for our honeymoon), Sri Lanka, and Las Vegas. All cancelled.

If I'm honest with myself, I must admit I was a tad relieved.

I felt my year had already been planned and scheduled for me before it had even started. Don't get me wrong; I am so grateful we are able to enjoy such luxuries. Once upon a time, that year's plans would have sounded like a pipe dream! But it also felt so organised with no room for magic, play, or spontaneity. (Or even room to just breathe.)

So, with an entire twelve months of nothing but white space in my calendar; a husband who still isn't ready for a baby; and me working from home and wanting something to cuddle, mother, and love, the universe aligned and had something better planned.

Finally, I got to welcome to our family a little fawn French bulldog. We called her Pumbaa!

If you're wondering why Pumbaa, yes, I named her after the warthog Pumbaa in *The Lion King*. I love his fun-loving nature, his loyalty, and her humorous run. (I don't know if you have seen a Frenchie run, but it's with a commitment and clumsiness that matches Pumbaa's distinctive locomotion.)

And, yes, she is a girl. But we live in the twenty-first century of breaking down gender stereotypes, right?

So what feels good? Puppy cuddles! That has to be universal, doesn't it? If a puppy doesn't make you smile and bring you joy, there has to be something seriously wrong with you.

So, I got to pick up our first fur baby this week. That's making me happy.

So, what else feels good?

Sex.

Duhh!

I am not sure if there is science behind it, if this is fact, or if this is just my personal experience, or if it's just an adult or a maturity thing. But, as I got older, I was involved in a relationship for seven years, and became more passionate and focused on business, sex kinda stopped taking up so much brain space. I thought that was probably normal.

Isn't it?

When you're in your early twenties and single, sex seems to occupy a lot of brain power, fuel a lot of conversations, and influence a lot of plans.

It's a frequent topic with girlfriends: Who's dating who? Did you go out on the weekend? Did you pick up? Did you sleep with him? Was the sex good? Are you going to do it again? Was it just a sex thing, or what happens next?

Then somewhere between there and here, conversations and mental space are consumed by new topics and issues. Discussions centre around careers, property, investments, travel, engagements, planning weddings, and starting families.

Sure we aren't in our fifties yet, and we're still young, so we kind of just assume everyone is having sex. But it's not really a thing we talk about anymore. We go to work, we make dinner, we have sex a few times a week. Right? Is that how this whole adult monogamous relationship life goes?

When I was catching up with my best friend in our hometown last week, we were laughing and reminiscing about our early-twenty-year-old selves and how reckless, fun, and fearless we were in the pursuit of quenching our sexual appetites.

We both were pretty outspoken feminists and had no shame in claiming or exploring our sexuality (she more so than I, and I am confident she will totally agree). I was always inspired by her "no-f#*ks-given" attitude and how she was never apologetic for standing in her power and her right to enjoy sex just as much as a man could without being "slut shamed."

But where had that fire, excitement, fun, and spontaneity gone?

Was that transition just part of the maturing journey? Is that what it means to now be an "adult" and "married"?

I used to have such a keen interest in gender psychology; in fact, I spent most of the six months studying abroad in Hawaii delving into this concept. I loved learning and understanding the evolution of women's sexuality and the difference in gender and sex psychology.

As you may know from my previous book, *Life Above Zero*, psychology is what inspires me and drives me. But I enjoy reading and learning about gender psychology and positive psychology specifically purely for enjoyment.

My girlfriend and I were exploring and teasing out society's model of what marriage is meant to look like and, personally, what it meant to both of us with reference to how marriage had been modelled to us through our own parents and the elders we looked up to in our own social circles. She mentioned a podcast she had listened to that had brought up some ideas that made her question and reconnect with her own sexuality and desires again.

This inspired me.

There was a spark of interest.

Curiosity.

Wonder.

Creativity.

Flow.

That quiet and soft tug again.

I hadn't felt that in a while. It reminded me of how much these topics, issues, science, and research used to intrigue me and how much enjoyment I found exploring them.

In the spirit of leaning in and following what feels good, I took this as a sign and, on my drive back to the Gold Coast last week, I listened to the podcast my girlfriend had mentioned.

I realised as I was listening that it was the first podcast I had listened to in a few years that had nothing to do with business, investing, or being productive. There was no intent to help me get closer to my goals.

I was listening purely because I was interested. I was listening purely for enjoyment.

I can't remember the last time I did this.

You know what? I don't even know the last time I read a book that didn't focus on personal and professional growth! So, I treated myself and bought the book that was publicised on the podcast. I wanted to learn more about women's sexuality and the need for adventure and novelty in order to keep monogamous, long-term relationships passionate and to provide mental space once again for the topic of sex.

Look at me go—rebelling and surrendering to what feels good.

Literally. Sex and a puppy!

Okay, guys. I've figured it out! All you other overachieving women out there, I've found the answer. Pour yourself a glass of wine and read a book because you enjoy it. Go buy yourself that puppy. Spice things up, get dressed up, treat yourself to some sexy lingerie, and have some hot sex with your hubby in a kinky place. Get that passion back!

That is how you slow down and get in tune with your flow and feminine energy again. The Surrender Project can end here!

If only it were that easy.

It might be? I'll keep you posted!

But, in all seriousness, as part of the Surrender Project, I have been consciously making time to write and connect with my intuition. I hope this inspires more downloads to come through.

Here's what I've picked up:

- I am feeling inspired to dress up, to feel good, and to feel sexy. I want to do my hair and do my makeup, which I usually only do when I'm filming content or going out for dinner or a night out.
- I have started allowing more white space in my day, allowing my day to not be so structured and rigid, making me feel obligated to complete certain tasks in certain time slots. I am trying to relax into my days, and the experience is slowly starting to feel more comfortable and less foreign and forced.
- I am realising I also have the desire to invest in homewares. (OMG—that's when you know you've become old!) I want my house to feel nice, or at least I want to invest and redecorate my study so I have a juicy safe space to sit and create and enjoy flow.

Chat soon.

Diary Entry 5

Got the puppy.

So it's been a week.

And considering these are *my* diary entries, I feel that this is the opportunity for me to be honest and tell you how I really feel.

Okay. I will admit that. I didn't realise a puppy would be this much work.

She is the cutest thing ever! I've definitely met my match when it comes to affection. (Touch is my love language.) She gives the best cuddles.

But I didn't realise how hands-on I'd have to be. She cries all night. She pisses and shits everywhere. If I can't watch her like a hawk to help with the potty training, I put her in her crate where she just cries some more.

I didn't know something so cute and quiet throughout the day could turn into a noisy high-pitched gremlin at night.

It's a full-time job!

Who was I kidding when I said I was ready to settle down and be a mum? If this is what it's like with a puppy, then I take it back. I am not ready for a human baby.

One thing on my side is that I haven't got much work I need to do or focus on right now. I'm honouring the promise of not taking on any new projects and outsourcing or automating most of the day-to-day stuff in my business before my Surrender Project, so I have the time.

But I totally underestimated the amount of time and energy this little fur child would demand from me.

I wonder if this is how a new mum feels when she explains that she is struggling but she would do it all over again because of how much she loves her child.

Would I do it all over again?

Honestly, I am not sure. But I can't admit that out loud to anyone. Especially my husband. He already thought a puppy was a bad idea. So, instead, I made it my idea and bought Pumbaa with my own money. So I can't give him the satisfaction of thinking he was right. I can't admit how challenged I am right now.

I was starting to harbour some feelings of resistance and resentment towards my husband. I was getting up at all hours of the night to comfort Pumbaa. I was constantly washing the towels and blankets she was pissing on. I would turn around after cleaning up one shit just to find she had done another one behind me. And I'd see Dan walking out the door to work letting me know "my dog" had pissed yet again. And he isn't even affectionate or nurturing towards her. I know he isn't a very affectionate man, naturally, but this is a puppy! Who doesn't want to love and cuddle a puppy? Had I married a psychopath?

Okay, so maybe he was right. And maybe having a puppy is a lot of work. And, yes, it isn't convenient. And, yes, it probably would be easier to toilet train a puppy when you have a backyard and don't live in an apartment.

But this is my Surrender Project. And it's the perfect time to train and love a puppy. I have nowhere to go, nowhere to be, and nothing to do.

And if my husband and I do want to have kids one day, well this has definitely been a good learning experience.

For me anyway.

I had realised and promised myself that, when it comes to kids, I would not be the one to try to influence or persuade Dan. I would wait until he came to me and said he is ready and one hundred per cent on board and excited about being a dad.

I know It's probably not fair to compare a puppy to a baby. But if this is "my" problem, then I would hate to know how much guilt I would feel if I had talked him into having a baby before he was ready. How sad to have a rude awakening after having a child. Sleepless nights, shitty nappies, and constant crying would all fall on me because it had been my idea.

We would both need to be in it one hundred per cent.

With the combination of my Surrender Project, writing and journaling again, reading books, and listening to podcasts about the evolution of human sexuality, I have been doing a lot of thinking and reflecting on marriage this week.

Is it fair to expect your partner to fill all roles—be your best friend, your protector, your partner in business and finances, the father of your children, your roommate, and also the hot sexy man who plays mind games with you in order to keep your deranged libido curious and turned on?

Is it fair for a woman to sacrifice her sexual pleasures and innate need for affection, novelty, and exciting sex because someone somewhere in the world decided once upon a time that monogamy was normal? That one person had to fulfil those needs for the rest of her life?

That sounds unrealistic and unnatural if you ask me. And more as if women need some form of formal agreement or a commitment that would be enforced by society and law that a man would take responsibility financially and emotionally for a child if his fun and games (orgasm) ended with responsibility (a child).

One thing I had promised Dan in our wedding vowels was that my happiness was my responsibility. He may be many things (and don't get me wrong—he is an amazing man, and that is why I married him), but I will never allow him to be responsible for my happiness or the sole source of it.

I had realised my emotions were also bubbling because I had neglected going outside this week. I had missed my exercise and meditation. (Reference A: the needy puppy.) But these activities are a massive piece to the puzzle of my sanity and my ability to be a vessel of compassion and light for myself and others.

I'm taking a mental note right now to think back on this when I am actually a mum to a human baby. I often hear mums I mentor in business struggling or feeling selfish if they dare to make some time for themselves—go to the gym or get a massage. But I also learned this week that, if I wanted to be a loving, positive, sane mum, I would need to be relentless in protecting my boundaries and making time for myself alone. Only then will I be able to be the best me and give the best of me (or at the very least, keep my kids alive and not hate everyone).

On that note, I put Pumbaa in her crate. I changed out of my pyjamas. I put on my activewear and headed down the beach for a walk for the first time in seven days. And I heard her cry as I left my street. I am such an evil mumma walking away as my baby cries. God, my neighbours must hate me!

I wonder if this is what mum guilt feels like? I have read that, when parents are "training" human babies to sleep through the night, they are actually not training the baby. They are training themselves. The parents. They are training themselves to sit in discomfort and the need for silence while they allow their babies to self-soothe.

It's so ironic that the very thing I had promised my husband I would never rely on him for—regulating my emotions—is the same lesson we try to instil in new-borns.

Where along the way do people fall into the illusion that their happiness is going to be found within something outside of themselves?

Pumbaa was definitely training and teaching me. She's forced me to sit in my discomfort. She's given me the opportunity for more joy and the space to reflect, sit in stillness, and question—a lot.

This week I have realised (or remembered) that I enjoy reading about sex and gender psychology. It's been a while since I involved myself in something because I just enjoyed learning about it. It was something I enjoyed in my degree too.

Is this my next tug or pull? Is this part of my destiny or path?

The entire point of this surrender experiment is to slow down and tune in so I can listen to my intuition and follow her guidance.

Is this her next nudge?

Diary Entry 6

The alternative therapies

AT THE START OF EVERY YEAR, I SET NEW YEAR GOALS. THESE ARE NOT so much resolutions or things I need to change, but things I want to experience and tick off the bucket list. Things I want to grow into being or achieve (if I am gifted with the next twelve months). I always acknowledge that the next twelve months aren't promised. Maybe that's why I am always trying to squeeze all the magic and juice out of them.

As I've said, nearly all my travel goals have been cancelled this pandemic year, and any that remain I have given up on for the year. But the pandemic has gifted me with more white space in which I can focus on other goals.

This year I wanted to have a kundalini experience, and I wanted to engage with a reiki healer. I believe in energy but have never investigated it or experienced it myself. So, in the spirit of my Surrender Project, slowing down and trying to tune in, I figured it was the perfect time to tick theses bad boys off my bucket list and do some further self and spiritual discovery.

One of my girlfriends recommended a kinesiologist who has always helped her when she didn't feel aligned or felt an energetic block and needed guidance with her next inspired step.

As you know, I am definitely spiritual; however, I'm still unsure what that looks like for me. So I was excited to explore this more, relinquish my control, and try to trust and surrender to faith instead.

I did try.

I know my aim was to trust and tap into believing rather than seeing. I wanted to lean further into my feminine being-and-trusting energy rather than my masculine doing-and-controlling energy. But my brain wouldn't let it go.

Throughout my reiki and kinesiology session, I found my logical brain judging and trying to rationalise and explain everything. I couldn't let go and believe that my body was actually talking and communicating with the kinesiologist.

It didn't make sense?

Sure. I guess I could believe that traumas are hidden and stored in the body.

I guess I also could believe that our bodies hold a natural intelligence about what is best for them. We shouldn't have to rely on something outside of us that thinks it knows what is best for us.

But was my body really telling the kinesiologist how many litres of water it needed? Was it telling her what affirmation I needed to hear from the angel card deck? Was it telling her what page of a certain book that she needed to read to prescribe me a certain dose of an essential oil?

I had to give myself a stern talking to. I had to chastise my inner critic for being such a judgmental bitch.

When it comes to the Surrender Project, I feel as if I am failing this test.

Nevertheless, despite my struggle to believe in what I could not see or hear myself, I tried to override my self-righteous judgments, lean in, and trust that what the kinesiologist was saying was what I needed to hear right now.

When she was touching my body, I felt she was applying the pressure that she was relying on in order to then label those exact movements as if my body was communicating with her (like a self-fulfilling prophecy). Although, I will admit that I did feel the energy move and shift within me when she didn't actually touch my body but hovered her hands over it.

There is magic and some sort of spirituality in that. Or maybe science?

But that further reinforced and reassured my belief in energy and that there has to be more than what meets the eye, more than what we can see or even explain.

Or maybe again that's my own self-confirmation bias trying to search for some certainty and my self-righteousness wanting to know it was right in believing there is more to life than "this."

Regardless, I kept giving myself pep talks and coercing myself to trust what the kinesiologist was advising and prescribing.

My body had communicated with her and told her that I needed to do the following:

- Drink one litre of water today.
- Drink one litre of water tomorrow before two in the afternoon.
- Moving forward, I needed to drink 2.5 litres daily.
- I am to repeat "I am now open to universal love" out loud eight times a day for two weeks.
- I need to focus on being "softer" and grounding into the present.
- I need to remind myself that the sun always shines on the earth, and it never asks for a thank you. I can do the same. I am deserving of universal love and abundance in all its forms, and I don't need to do anything in order to earn it.

- I need to continue to seek proof of the abundance always flowing around me. I must observe it in nature and in people who work and create money and success easily. There is evidence that such a revelation can change my current belief systems.
- I needed to check in with my older self and ask, "What would she say to me?"

I had a little chuckle at this one, realising I was paying someone to give me my own advice.

If you read my previous book, you would know about the rocking chair test in which you time-travel to your eighty-year-old self and check in with what advice she would give you to help you get perspective when navigating muddy, unclear waters.

But I gave myself another stern talking to and told myself off for being so self-righteous. I instructed my know-it-all self to listen and be a student. I don't know everything, and obviously I am not taking my own advice; otherwise, I wouldn't be here paying someone else to give it to me.

I need to listen.

I know nothing.

I am here to listen and learn.

I am here to surrender and trust.

The kinesiologist further advised me that I needed to check in with myself daily and ask, "What could I do today that would feel good?"

I was already answering that in my head. I needed to read, write, have a bath, have sex, get a massage, and bask in the delicious smell of essential oils.

She passed on that I needed to buy the essential oil called "whisper." It would help tap into my feminine. She also advised me to put three drops of the oil known as "mountain devil" under my tongue at least once daily until the bottle is empty. Mountain devil is apparently used to transform anger, hatred, and jealousy into unconditional love and forgiveness.

What came up that I did find interesting was apparently a block I had in accepting abundance and allowing myself to receive. This also came in the form of compliments.

I guess I have resistance towards praise because I don't feel as if we should need praise, accolades, or recognition to encourage us to do something. We should do things for ourselves despite who may or may not be watching.

I wrote about this in *Life Above Zero*—the need to be congruent and how consistency speaks volumes about our character. And I guess this feeds into my discomfort around compliments. I always feel this way: "Thank you, but I was going to do this and achieve this anyway. I don't need the pat on the back, and I didn't do this so I could receive your validation."

But the kinesiologist explained it differently. She said it's more like a flower. It shines brightly and does its thing regardless of anything around it because it's just in its nature to bloom and flourish. But people still admire her beauty. Allow them to. It doesn't detract from our mission or dilute our drive. It makes us feel good to be able to admire and bask in its beauty and gifts, so allow yourself to receive it. Accept it.

Who are you to cheat them out of that satisfaction of admiring the beauty they see?

It definitely gave me more to think about, and a new way of thinking about things as I drove home.

I don't know if I passed that test with flying colours. Despite the few times I had to pull myself up and send my logical brain to the naughty corner for taking over the show, I still felt the resistance.

I think the judgey judge within me struggled to fully surrender and believe. But I was open to explore the new concepts and allow the messages the kinesiologist had passed on to sink in.

Diary Entry 7

What feels good?

THE GOOD SCHOOLGIRL IN ME WAS ALREADY STARTING ON THE HOMEWORK the kinesiologist had given me.

I have always been like that. That has always been one of my traits that I do appreciate. You might call it loyalty, productivity, reliability, integrity. Regardless of what you label it, if I say I'm going to do something or be somewhere, you can count on me. You don't need to remind me or check in.

There is something that just doesn't sit right with me when people say they're going to do something (whether it's a commitment to self or someone else) and they don't follow through.

I've realised that this is what also leads to self-confidence and people's belief and confidence in us. If we continue to let ourselves down, we start to feel useless and worthless. No matter how small the commitment is, show up and honour it for your own self-worth.

I show up. In every aspect of my life.

I don't always arrive with amazing quality or results or with great poise. Sometimes it's messy, scattered, and with some neglect for the finer details. But I always try.

What was that?

Unconsciously, am I trying to get a pat on the back? That praise I claimed I apparently didn't enjoy or chase consciously—has that been driving me unconsciously for years?

Where did that come from?

I was going through all my old school reports the other day whilst cleaning out our cupboard, and I was curious: At what point in my life had I started becoming a human doing? How old was I when the belief was instilled in me that I needed to work hard and achieve and constantly be striving?

I realised whilst reading my reports that nearly every teacher, every term of every year of primary and high school, referred to me as conscientious.

What the hell does that even mean?

Was it a cop-out? A word that would excuse them from actually having to say anything personalised and elaborate? How is it that we, as kids, had to write thousands of words in class to prove our worth and be judged and scored on, yet the teachers got away with a measly one or two sentences to summarise our efforts, performances, and abilities? Most of the reports about me included the word *conscientious*.

Well, this conscientious adult now has to look up what that word even means fifteen years on. If I don't know what it means at the age of twenty-eight, I definitely didn't know what it meant at the age of twelve, so conscientiousness wasn't something I was consciously trying to do, be, or have written on my scorecard.

A quick internet search informed me that conscientiousness is the personality trait of being careful or diligent. Conscientiousness implies a desire to do a task well and to take obligations to others seriously. Conscientious people tend to be efficient and organised as opposed to easy going and disorderly.

Okay. Yep. That's me.

How is it they just summarised my last page in one word?

Even back when I was a child, I was focused on doing and completing tasks well!

Did that result from nature or my nurture?

Everything I had learned about psychology and happiness had explained that real happiness is experienced in "flow," which can only be created when we're in a situation in which we are being stretched. Happiness is found in growing. If we aren't growing, we are stuck. We feel stagnant, in a rut. Goals and growth are pivotal; they are required if we are to experience fulfilment and happiness. But we have to have the required skills to reach our goals. The goals must stretch us but still be achievable; otherwise, we feel overwhelmed, anxious, and helpless. Likewise, if the goals are too easy, we feel bored, depressed, and unfulfilled.

So, maybe I had just unknowingly mastered this lesson at an early age, and that was why I was always running a million miles per hour, always stretching myself, achieving, and often described as a positive and happy-go-lucky person.

A child genius or just a complete fruit loop?

I'll let you decide.

The whole point of this Surrender Project is to try to stop judging and giving everything meaning. It is just to surrender to being. So I'll abandon this quest for answers for now and divert back to the task of leaning into what feels good.

Without judgement, I try to tune into my intuition, to hear my inner truth or guidance, She whispers to me:

So for once in my life, "doing" does not feel good.

I am being called to relax. Actually it's more like I am being demanded to relax.

I want to find a new space or apartment. Somewhere with new energy. I want lots of natural light. I want my own study—a sacred room full of juicy positive jujus where I can sit, create, and experience magic. I want a spare bedroom where family members can stay when they visit. Eventually it will be for a new human baby. I want a backyard for Pumbaa and grass so I can ground myself and sit in the sunshine daily. I want to be close to the beach for my morning walks and afternoon runs. And I want an entertaining area so I can have the girls I mentor in business over for community and connection, soul chats, and girl time over cocktails.

I will contribute to sex and gender psychology research, but for now, I will just explore it and allow it to bring me joy and curiosity.

I will document everything I am learning right now as I navigate my next pivot and up-level in business; income; and impact in terms of marketing, branding, and designing a career that brings me joy because I will teach it and, in exchange, will receive wealth from it. It will end up being a piece of my business and will enable other thought leaders to share their message and continue to help raise the vibration and consciousness of the world.

Also, I will pursue a masters and a PhD. There is more study in psychology to come with research contributing to and exploring feminism, sex, and gender psychology, female empowerment, the impact of relationship and resilience that faith has on mental health.

Yep.

That vision feels good.

I can definitely lean into that.

That feels aligned and what I want right now.

But can I trust that it will manifest? Without me hustling for it now?

How can I act on that when I'm not supposed to be doing anything? I promised to surrender and not hustle or force.

But I can flow.

And right now I am feeling that flow again as I write. I am journaling and writing most mornings for a couple of hours now.

And—you can't win the lottery if you don't have a ticket, right? So, I trust the universe will work its magic, but I also need to show up. I promise no force or pressure. I'm just going to start looking for new apartments online and see if any come up that feel aligned with my vision. When we were in the process of buying our last apartment three years ago, everything felt difficult for six months. We were putting in offers and getting knockback after knockback. But the one we are in now is exactly what we were looking for. It even matched the picture on my vision board! We got it for the exact price we had in our budget. There were no competitive offers. And we didn't budge with a counteroffer. It came with ease and flow.

So right now, my next aligned action or my intuition is guiding me to look for a new home and continue to write.

That I can do. That flows and feels good.

One of my girlfriends gave me a doobie when I was home last week, to force me to chill the f#*k out. I'm not a stoner, let me add. Not that I have any judgement of those who are. Even when I was working in child protection, I came to believe (as most of my colleagues did) that there is no harm in recreational drug use as long as it doesn't affect any other areas of your life, like work, relationships, parenting, health, and so forth. If you have kids and you organise them to be looked after by someone else whilst you are out under the influence, and you are in a safe environment and putting no one else at risk—no judgement here.

Why is it that most of society is okay with alcohol despite the fact that most accidents and acts of violence are fuelled by intoxication? Alcohol is a drug too.

People have been using drugs for centuries to tap into different levels of consciousness and alter their state. Think about coffee! I bet societal attitudes would change if other drugs were legalised. And what I mean by legalised is that the government collects taxes from the sales. Legalisation would lead to education, monitoring, and regulation, all of which would provide safety for manufacturers and users alike. Anyway, that's a war for someone else to fight. One battle and quest at a time, girlfriend.

So back to my doobie. In the spirit of what feels good, my two younger brothers were over for dinner, and we were playing the Monopoly card game. I suggested that, for shits and giggles, we should get high.

One of my brothers, Will, is an accountant; one who does things by the books let me add. So I'll let that speak for itself. He was reluctant. But I, along with my ratbag brother, Rhys, are pretty good at twisting his arm. So next thing I knew we were all in hysterics sitting on my balcony laughing at who knows what.

Actually, I'm pretty sure Rhys and I were laughing at Will. Not hurting a fly.

My stomach did hurt, though, from laughing so much. My heart was so full as I relished in the gratitude I have for my two not-so-little brothers and the joy and love they bring into my life.

Note to self: It really is the small things in life (and a doobie).

Diary Entry 8

Being present

THE KINESIOLOGIST SUGGESTED THAT I TRY TO INCORPORATE MORE mindfulness into my life.

Being present.

I actually used to do this naturally every day.

Her suggestion inspired me to look back on the periods when I experienced the most joy in my life, and I realised that, during those times, I was soaking everything in and practising mindfulness.

I know the term *mindfulness* is thrown around like some New Age medicine that hippies use, but for me, it's been a pretty simple and powerful way to shift my focus, expand time, and maximise joy.

My experience of mindfulness goes like this: I am in a moment and allowing myself to be really in it while, at the same time, I'm taking more of a third-person gaze and having an out-of-body experience. It's hard to explain, but it's as if my consciousness or spirit elevates and observes the experience (and myself in it) as a third person. I am gifted with the unique experience of being able to see and feel it all and take a mental picture at the same time.

Even now, I can recall moments in which I have felt so freaking grateful, joyful, and full of abundance because I took an extra few seconds to be present and take the whole moment in—being mindful of all the sensual pleasures.

And It's just little moments.

When I was sixteen, my girlfriends and I were walking across the oval across the road from my house with bottles of Passion Pop in hand. I remember the waves and thick fringe we had just spent the last hour perfecting with our hair spray and triple barrel curling wand. I remember the smell of Marc Jacobs Daisy perfume. I remember loving Daylight Savings; despite the late hour, we were still enjoying a bit of extra sunshine. I danced and flirted with the balmy warm summer air; there was a hint of wonder in it. I experienced a feeling of excitement not knowing where the night would take us. I remember the Kings of Leon song "Sex Is on Fire" playing in my head and feeling as if we would be forever young.

I experienced another mindful moment when a sexy, mysterious, tall man (my husband now) picked me up from the airport after I'd been travelling in Europe for a month. Even though his greeting hug lasted for probably only a few seconds, I remember taking it all in. I remember his warm chest pressed against mine. I remember how good he smelled. I remember thinking, *F#★k! I think I am falling for this man!* I remember how happy I felt to be home. How excited I was to get to know and explore this man. How safe I felt in his arms and how grateful I felt to have someone who missed and cared about me and didn't want me to get public transport back to the Gold Coast by myself late at night.

I will always remember the cuddle I gave my mum after she had a heart attack. I had thought we were going to lose her. I remember holding her hand and taking it all in, remembering exactly what her hands looked like. I remember looking deep into her eyes and how much love I found in them. I remember her smell. It is the sort of smell

I think we take for granted, but to me it represented twenty-eight years of comfort. I remember breathing in her scent as if it was a drug I was trying to get high off, with the realisation I nearly never got to enjoy or seek retreat in that smell ever again. I remember cuddling her and thinking I would never ask for anything ever again because I was the luckiest and wealthiest girl alive. The angels/the universe/god answered my prayers and brought her back to us.

Why haven't I allowed myself to continue to feel that gratitude every day?

Maybe it's like happiness. We habituate, adapt, and forget our blessings unless we take time to remember how quickly they can be taken from us.

When I was at university (and I was a poor university student), one night a girlfriend and I took ourselves out for dinner. Instead of eating the typical eggs or beans on toast, we brought our own bottle of wine (a $10 one may I add) and ordered a marinara pasta at a fancy restaurant. I look back now and realise it wasn't fancy at all, but we truly believed we were fancy! I remember how good the pasta tasted, the smell of the parmesan cheese, and the crispiness of the white wine as it refreshed my palette between mouthfuls of garlic. I remember thinking how grateful I was. How abundant my life was. How wealthy I was. And how I had made it! I had moved to the Gold Coast. I was supporting myself, and I was so lucky that I could afford to treat myself to a dinner at a restaurant.

When did I stop being so freaking grateful? Why do I not savour every mouthful when I eat out now? When did I stop acknowledging the abundance that enables me do treat myself to dinner or breakfast out most weekends? When did that stop being a luxury and just something I take for granted?

I am so freaking lucky.

My life is so f#*king abundant.

I am blessed every day.

I have been ungrateful and have stopped making the time to not only count my blessings but to spend a few extra seconds really enjoying them.

So, when I cuddled Pumbaa this morning, I took it all in: Her soft coat. Her cute puppy smell. Her adorable little paws that love resting in my hands. Her little heartbeat that beats next to mine. (She's like my own personal hot water bottle.) Her little beady brown eyes that look at me so helplessly. How could one little puppy bring me so much love? Within just ten seconds of giving myself permission to be present and mindful of all my emotions and senses, my heart was filled up so much it could have exploded. I just look at her and want to squish her.

I am not psychotic, I swear. Apparently, social psychology researchers have done studies that explain that the reason we feel as if we want to squeeze cute things is that seeing the cuteness causes aggression. So, when you see a cute dog or a new baby or even a person you find unbelievably adorable, your brain is forced to become really aggressive, and you might want to squeeze the object of your emotion to death. The cuter the thing you're looking at, the more frustrated you become. Oddly, there is a name for this phenomenon: cute aggression.

So yep, I am not psychotic. We humans are. No wonder we have such a hard time working ourselves out.

We are f#*king crazy!

But I promise not to squeeze Pumbaa to death. I will step away from the puppy and put her back in her crate and go for that beach walk I promised myself I would prioritise every day. The sun is warm as it kisses my face. The smell of the salt in the air reminds me of family holidays we enjoyed when I was growing up when I explored jetties and chatted to fishermen with my brothers. The sound of the waves rolling in and slipping away soothes my soul as if I were listening to the cooing from a seashell. The metallic blue glistens with peaks of silver and reminds me of the magic that is found just sitting in the stillness of Mother Nature. It always feels like a different pace down there. Everything slows down, yet I trust that everything is right on time. I took a deep breath of abundance and exhaled gratitude as I sat in the sun's warm hug a little longer.

That night I made a conscious effort to practise mindfulness as I got into bed and nestled myself under Dan's chin like I usually do. But somewhere along the way, I had stopped taking the few extra seconds to be grateful for it. I always marvelled at how our bodies fit so snug together—like puzzle pieces. It's as if we had always been destined to find each other. His chin on my forehead, my head on his shoulder, my hip hugged into his waist, his legs between my thighs, and my legs wrapped around his body. I have always felt at home when I am with him. No matter what bed we are sleeping in, in what country, or what language I can hear being spoken outside the window, home is where he is. He has a way of calming me and making me feel safe. He is the calm to my crazy. This has always been my favourite part of the day— crawling into bed with him and getting cuddles. And he always smells so good! Even after he has just jumped out of the shower and is not wearing cologne, his bare skin smells so yummy. I've heard on the grapevine that, apparently, this means we are meant to have the best babies!

No, but seriously! Apparently hidden in a man's smell/pheromones are clues about his major histocompatibility complex (MHC) genes and a woman's genetic compatibility with him. Studies suggest that we women prefer the scent of males whose MHC genes differ from our own, a preference that has probably evolved because it helps our offspring survive. Couples with different MHC genes are less likely to be related to each other than couples with similar genes. Children of couples with different MHC genes are born with more varied

MHC profiles, which means healthier babies with better immune systems.

See? We are all just wild animals, sniffing each other out looking for a mate to make the best babies with. Why do we try to fool each other with all the courting, manners, morals, and mind games?

"You and me baby ain't nothin' but mammals, so let's do it like they do on the Discovery Channel!"[1]

Animal or human instinct—either way, I snuggled into him a little tighter, breathed him in a little deeper, and tried to stay awake a little longer, taking him all in and counting all my blessings before floating off to sleep.

I really need to start journaling in my gratitude journal each night again, making time to recognise and count my blessings as well as creating the space to make magic and be grateful for what hasn't arrived yet … tapping into manifestation and visualisation, and allowing myself to experience those feelings now.

I will start that tomorrow.

Some late-night afterthoughts:

I have been trusting the pull and leaning into the universe's coercion (even when it was uncomfortable). I felt some nudges from the universe this week, and rather than judging, resisting, or doubting, I trusted. I responded to some emails and applied for an on-stage speaking gig for the success resources event as well as an alumni award for Griffith University.

I reminded myself to relinquish control, follow the breadcrumbs, surrender to faith.

What's next? Where am I being pulled to go?

I'm a vessel for good. I am open. And I trust.

After today's little experiment and with some extra context with what's happening in the world right now—world pandemic, global

---

[1] From a song entitled "The Bad Touch" by the Bloodhound Gang.

financial crises, and the Black Lives Matter movement—I felt fuelled and fired up. With all the blessings the majority of us have in this Western world, who are we not to be happy? Who are we not to be successful? Who are we not to chase our dreams? Who are we not to show up for ourselves and prove to ourselves and others that we can create whatever we dream?

If I have learned anything from my experiences in 2020, it is that the majority of us are very privileged. We have more opportunity, resources and enjoy a standard of living not even royalty did not that long ago.

We can't take our privilege for granted or feel guilty for making the time to enjoy it.

We *owe* it to the people who don't have the opportunities and privileges we have to be happy and fulfil those big dreams in our hearts and stop playing small.

To me, that's injustice. Not using or maximising the gifts and privileges we have been given just reflects ignorance.

But that's my TED talk for today. Now It's time to return to basking in my blessings in this yummy man's arms.

Diary Entry 9

Okay. I'll admit it. I got triggered

OKAY. SO I GOT TRIGGERED.

Good friends of mine made twenty thousand dollars overnight. I don't know why, but it pissed me off. And considering these are my journal entries, I am allowed to be honest. I'm not saying I'm right or justified. But this news triggered me.

So, I am sitting here trying to unpack it.

Yes, I am happy for them.

And, yes, I know conceptually that their success is not another's failure. And I know that does not mean there is less money for anyone else, because money is abundant and is an unlimited resource (especially in 2020 it feels as if the Australian government just keeps printing more anyway without any consequences to deal with the financial crises and world pandemic).

Maybe it's jealousy?

I had to bust my butt to create wealth. It was slow, hard work. It was compounding after years of hustle. And theirs just flowed in. Overnight! Actually, more like it "hailed" in!

I know this is the proof I need to change my belief about having to work hard for money. And it's more evidence to prove the contrary.

I know I have to give this a new meaning.

But it still doesn't change my innate response. My emotional response was almost immediate and happened even before I had time to rationalise it or regulate my emotions.

Sure, I smiled and tried to show I was happy for them. But I couldn't help but harbour my own feelings of defeat. Then guilt. Then greed.

Why not me? Why them? They already have so much money, and I don't see them working hard for it.

Don't be such a negative, selfish bitch, Lauren. Be happy for your friends and get out of your scarcity mindset! You know they have worked hard in the past. They are just ten years of "work" ahead of you.

Don't be so ungrateful. You're already so blessed. You already have such an abundant life. When are you going to be happy with what you already have?

No matter how much back-and-forth chatter was going on in my head between my inner mean girl and my rational, sensible, and unbiased self, they couldn't get to a point of understanding or agreement.

I tried to sit there and just observe the inner chatter as an innocent bystander while my crazy voices tried to hash it out. But it was tiring listening to them argue. It left me drained with no mental capacity for inspiration or productivity.

There was no gas left in the tank to fuel me for the day, and it was only eleven in the morning!

I couldn't will, push, or guilt-trip myself into doing any work.

So I didn't.

I gave myself permission to have a "me day."

If I am honest, I have probably only given myself two of these days in the last four years (not including weekends or holidays). People who are employees throw in a "sickie" now and then when they need a "me day." I guess that's the difference between the entrepreneur and the employee mindset. I know some places are calling them mental health days now.

I didn't have the opportunity to try to come up with an extravagant story to explain why I couldn't come to work today. I had an internal conversation with myself and justified why I needed one of those days. And my boss gave me permission to sit on my ass today. (She's so awesome!)

So I did.

I sat on the couch. I watched movies. And I cuddled my dog.

I felt so freaking emotional. I had to check to see that I wasn't due for my period because those were waves of emotions I was still only just getting used to after coming off contraception this year after ten years of suppressing that feminine wisdom too.

No luck.

So I couldn't even blame my tantrum on my hormones. It was all due to my shitty beliefs, and I needed to sit with them and rewire them.

And I had to do this without making myself right or wrong. I tried to resist putting my judgey judge hat on and instead be inquisitive and compassionate with myself—the way I am when I am coaching and working with one of my private clients.

I came back to the questions: What would feel good today? What feels like the next aligned step?

Recently I have been finding comfort, guidance, and clarity by turning to my angel cards and reading a page out of the book *A Course in Miracles* by Helen Schucman because I know strategy, logic, and rationale have got me to where I am today, but they are not going to get me where I want to go mentally, spiritually, and financially.

I was ready to surrender to something else.

I pulled the home card from my angel deck. The Angel Muriel advised me:

This may be a time where greater attention is placed on the home and what this means to you. This is the time for reflecting on your foundations and cleaning out the debris. Through connecting to our home space we experience a greater sense of connection to ourselves.

This is the time to clean and clear out the old and stagnant energies and put the time and love you deserve into having the kind of physical space that truly supports and nourishes you on all levels of your being.

It may also be time to let go of your old belief systems around the concept of home. Home is where the heart is. It is the space of love, nourishment and support. No matter where you are, who you are with or where you live, you carry home in your heart as you walk through this planet which is your home.[2]

Interesting, considering I had been looking into either moving into a new home or redecorating my study.

The page I read today in *A Course in Miracles* was entitled: "Don't get even, get odd." Lesson five explained that I am never upset for the reason I think I am. It might seem as if I'm upset because of something happening "out there," but a hundred per cent of the time, I'm upset because of something that is happening within me. Life itself is never painful. It's simply a mirror of my beliefs. I can't really fix my problems "out there." That would be like looking in the mirror and noticing my mascara is smudged and then trying to fix it by wiping the mirror. I must fix my problems by recognising them as a case of mistaken identity and then changing the inner belief, the inner cause.

---

[2] Carisa Mellado, Ask An Angel (Victoria, Australia: Blue Angel Publishing, 2012).

I have been instructed three or four times today to search my mind for a sort of upset, worry, fear, or depression and to simply acknowledge that, no matter its facade, its cause is not what I think. Instead of getting even with that problem that appears to be out there, I am encouraged to get odd by going inside and knowing that, despite all appearances, the universe is just saying "I love you." I am the one giving it a different meaning.

I looked up after reading the page and saw it was 4:11 pm. Angel numbers. I felt a weight lift off my shoulders, and I heaved a sigh of relief knowing that I wasn't alone. Despite being uncomfortable and being forced to reflect within and look at my unpretty parts, I was being guided. I was on the right path.

I leaned into what felt good and trusted that my body wanted to be moved, and it needed some extra loving. So I lifted myself off the couch and took myself for a walk to stir the stagnant energy that had been sitting heavy in my body all day. It felt as if my mind had just done a good job of shifting through its shit, and it was encouraging me to take out the trash.

So, I listened. I trusted and treated myself to some fresh air and ocean medicine.

On my walk, I felt as if my mind wanted to retreat from the heaviness of being a "shrink" listening to all my shit today. It wanted a break from having to solve all the world's (my) problems. It was more interested in entertaining the thoughts of whether I should get Botox.

Isn't it funny? When our heads are not preoccupied with goals or with higher visions or missions, they have space for more shallow and pretentious desires.

It's kind of like psychologist Abraham Maslow's hierarchy of needs theory of motivation; once you have your physical needs met (water, shelter, food, and clothing), you worry about your safety needs. Once your safety needs are met (employment, resources, health), you worry about your love and belonging. Once your love and belonging needs are met (intimacy, family, friends, and sense of connection), you worry about your esteem. Once your esteem needs are met (respect, status, recognition, freedom), you then worry about self-actualisation. Once your self-actualisation needs are met (the desire to become the most that one can be), I guess you're free to worry about whatever the f#★k you want.

What a luxury it is to have all my needs met and to be afforded the mental capacity to worry or to wonder if Botox is a good idea.

I can't help but be curious—has this got anything to do with the mental health crisis we are experiencing in the Western world at the moment? In the twenty-first century, so many of us live better than royalty did not that long ago. Rather than having to worry where our next meal is going to come from or where we will sleep today, we have spare time to ponder. Are we really happy? Are we reaching our full potential? Could we do better?

What luxury we have, yet it can be a curse of misery.

Diary Entry 10

Surrendering isn't giving up

WITHOUT A CLEAR GOAL TO WORK TOWARDS OR A LAID-OUT ACTION plan, I can't find a way to get myself there. It's fair to say not only do I feel out of my comfort zone, but I feel as if I am not in a zone at all. I feel as if I'm not moving. As if I am not being active in the process and as if I am giving up.

Sure, every day I am still doing the day-to-day things I usually do to run my business (minus a lot of the stuff I outsourced or automated). So it's not as if I am sitting on my ass. I am just not hungry and hustling towards something specific.

I understand we can't be on the go 24/7. And life and business happen in seasons. But what's the purpose of this season I am navigating?

Is it just to rest?

Should I be doing something?

As part of my morning routine and everyday ritual, I move, meditate, then nourish my body with plant-based nutrition support.

This morning I tuned into a meditation that was about learning how to trust. And almost immediately after I finished, I felt a clearing or unblocking. I felt energy start to freely and calmly flow from my sacral chakra to my heart chakra and then float to my crown chakra (which is an energy channel that felt stagnant before).

I was reminded that self-love is needed to raise our vibrations. All I need to be doing right now is trust my intuition, take inspired action when I'm being guided to, and be in charge of my state.

Self-love is how I do that. Radical self-love is how you take responsibility for your state, the frequency you're vibrating at, and in turn, the opportunities you manifest or things you attract.

It's crazy. Before the meditation, I felt antsy, anxious, agitated, and frustrated. And within fifteen minutes I felt grounded and in control. I trusted that everything was happening at the perfect time.

Because of the pandemic, it took twelve months to get my book, *Life Above Zero*, published and out in books stores and on different platforms. It finally launched on Audible this week. I got a call from my publisher that Brumby Sunstate, the leading Australian wholesaler of books, had also picked up my book this week, so bookstores would be able to start ordering it from their catalogues and stocking their shelves.

I took a breath. My book was no longer in my hands, and I reminded myself that I didn't need to push or pursue anything. I just needed to trust. Relinquish control. Surrender to faith. And allow joy.

I am on purpose and on time.

What feels good right now is taking that self-love to the next level and consequently raising my vibration in the process.

I decided to focus on my health, radiance, and vitality again with good nutrition, lots of water, minimal alcohol (because, let's be honest, margaritas are good for the soul on a Sunday afternoon), conscious movement, and lots of sleep and rest.

That goes for my business too. I'm going to focus and change my messaging back to health and just sharing what I am personally doing and what's been helping me with my own health and happiness—putting myself first and being an example for other women who are recovering human doings too and who need permission to take time for themselves—without the guilt!

How funny are we humans? We live with so much societal pressure to be good people and help others when they need it, volunteering our time and money. But should we feel guilty or selfish if we invest our time and money to help ourselves? (This, may I add, also helps others and prevents us being a burden on others so they can free up their resources to help themselves too.)

So here I am. Still committing to surrendering. I have an idea of where I want to go, but I'm letting go of the details and surrendering the "how" I am going to get there to something bigger than me. Because, if I am honest, I must say I am tired of trying to control and force everything.

Plus, this is more fun.

What is going to happen next when I trust?

Note: I booked the Botox for my frown lines! I still can't believe I did it, mostly because I am terrified of needles so I can't believe I would willingly volunteer myself as a cushion to be pricked! I hosted a girls' night last night, and some of the women I mentor in business (who have become close friends) were telling me, over some cheeky wines, that they have been getting it done for years.

I had a little chuckle to myself at how we women compare ourselves to others without realising that we have no chance to change ourselves to look like them. A lot of us compare ourselves to something that is physically impossible. No amount of hydration, veggies, sunscreen, or skin products you see models sharing on Instagram is going to make you look like the women who are sharing them. Sure, all these routines help; they are great for your skin and overall health, but as I have been learning, most of the women we compare ourselves to have been getting Botox! Why spend $250 on anti-ageing products that you *hope* might make a difference in a few months when you could pay $150 and get an immediate, guaranteed result?

I used to think of it as pretentious. But now, after looking into it, I think it is a smart return on your investment! Besides, what's the difference between anti-ageing products and makeup and a few injections in your face? Both are not natural, and both are meant to enhance your physical appearance. Where do we draw the line?

If only more women were open about what they were doing cosmetically, maybe other women wouldn't beat themselves up comparing themselves to something that is simply unrealistic. Either pay to have the work done or love your natural beauty and ageing. There is no need to beat yourself up and compare real grass to fake turf. They are two different things that look distinctively different, not variants of the same.

What feels best for you? What are you willing to invest to maintain and look after what you want?

In the spirit of radical self-love, I am letting go of my judgement. I am not telling my husband (or getting his approval, opinion, or validation). I am doing what I want to do and what makes me feel good. Botox, here I come!

Diary Entry 11

Teaching a dog new tricks

SINCE I AUTOMATED AND OUTSOURCED ALL THE AREAS OF MY BUSINESS that didn't bring me joy and could be delegated, it's crazy how much "white space" I now have.

This is what I spent the last four years hustling and working hard for: time.

Only three years ago, lack of time was my biggest excuse for so many things; I felt that there just wasn't enough of it to get everything done on my to-do list. And that list was keeping me on track for my goals. And here I am now with endless amounts of time. I'm free to spend it any way I like.

What's even more interesting is that I have found that time expands for me now. I always have more than enough time to enjoy or complete things.

I kind of manifested this Surrender Project at the start of the year when I was doing my annual reflection of the past year and setting new goals for 2020. (I don't think any of us knew what a doosey this year was going to be!) One of my goals was to not only create more white space but to *enjoy* it.

I have actually written down these goals: Create white space every day for stillness. Rejoice in life. Accept and receive all the pleasure life has to offer. Allow life to be easy and overflowing with joy and abundance.

I posted them on my bathroom mirror.

It sounds pretty woo-woo and airy-fairy, I know! But I was really deliberate in the language I used after reading Louise Hay's book *You Can Heal Your Life* over the Christmas break.

I twisted my ankle a few days before my wedding (which was a week before Christmas). I was supposed to be clocked off and in holiday mode, but I felt restless and guilty for sitting on my ass, so I decided to go for a big run. And *bam!* There went my ankle.

It wasn't as if I needed it to walk down the aisle or dance all night in heels anyway!

As I was reading *You Can Heal Your Life*, I had a little chuckle to myself because, apparently, injured ankles are related to "resistance or guilt around enjoying and accepting all the pleasure life has to offer." [3] This rang so true for me then (as it still does now) as I struggled to relax and slow down without feeling guilty.

So, ironically, here I am, halfway through 2020. I have the longed-for white space, and now I'm being challenged to figure out how to enjoy it.

I guess we'd better be careful what we wish for!

Today I spent a couple of hours on calls with women I am mentoring in business. But to be honest, it doesn't feel like work. I love catching up with them. They are women I love chatting to, women I vibe with. My work with them feels like just catching up and having deep and meaningful conversations with friends talking about mindset, business,

---

[3] Louise Hay, *You Can Heal Your Life* (Carlsbad, California: Hay House, Incorporated, 1999), 212.

leadership, wealth, and health (which are things I am passionate about and would talk about in my spare time anyway).

And the best bit is that I didn't have to hustle to find these girls to coach or mentor. I attracted them to me by being me, sharing my message and mission, and investing in marketing, which was a new level I consciously chose to step up into this year.

Isn't that what marketing is? Leveraging time?

I've heard there are three currencies: money, time, and relationships/audience.

We need to have at least two to be able to create the third. If we have time and relationships, we can leverage them to create money. If we have money and time, we can leverage them to create influential relationships and strategic partnerships—an audience. If we have relationships/an audience and money, we can leverage them to create time.

I guess I've spent the last four years building relationships and money, so now I can buy more time. Marketing and outsourcing take a lot of the hustle and woman-hours out of my business. But I could only buy that initially with time as I built up my other two banks.

So, I need to be okay with that. It's not as if I am not working; It's just that I have marketing systems and people working on my behalf.

I need to trust that.

I am moving.

But, why is it that I have such a hard time accepting that?

I caught myself today looking for things to do to fill my time and be productive. So I stopped and gave myself permission to shut down my computer halfway through the afternoon on a Tuesday to be present and play with Pumbaa and try to teach her some new tricks.

I have been trying to teach her how to sit and stay. I've enjoyed learning how to teach her. I think it's because the methods have a lot to do with psychology and the realisation that we humans aren't all that different to animals. To form a new habit, the new habit has to be convenient, have a cue that is accessible (and visible if it isn't), and takes effort. Humans as well as dogs need their behaviour to be reinforced with a reward. It makes us feel like the bee's knees and makes it worth going out of our conditioned behaviours to do it again.

Dogs (and humans) are more receptive to positive reinforcement than punishment. Because when we feel good, we do good. And we do it over and over again because we want people to see how amazing we are. Sometimes we are punished, which makes us feel embarrassed, ashamed, or worthless. But that doesn't necessarily stop us from doing the "wrong" thing again. It just encourages us to make sure that, when we do that undesirable behaviour again, we do it in private (like pissing in the spare room on the carpet where we won't get in trouble because our human doesn't see us).

But we humans are then left to suffer in silence with our own self-loathing and guilt without the support. Because no one knows what we are doing, and we don't talk about it with others. So we don't realise we aren't alone in what we are going through, and we are all just pissing in our spare rooms but too embarrassed to admit it.

I love that Pumbaa's little brain is a clean slate and all mushy, ready to be wired and moulded the way I want her to be and behave.

She is like my own little experiment.

Is that messed up?

Although I am experimenting with how I teach her and bring her up, she is probably teaching me more than I am teaching her. She has already taught me (or forced me) to slow down, be present, and allow joy.

I feel like a little child playing again.

If only I had a trainer teaching me new tricks and reinforcing my good behaviour with treats every time I did something good and calling me out when I pissed on the floorboards so I wouldn't do it again. Wouldn't we all be good little humans!

In the meantime, I've spent the last hour talking to my puppy in a baby voice and chasing her around the apartment. And now I am about to make a yummy plant-based shake (because real self-love starts with how we nourish our bodies, and I am all about that right now). Then I will sit on the couch and spend the rest of my afternoon reading *Sex at Dawn: How We Mate, Why We Stray, and What It Means* by Cacilda Jethá and Christopher Ryan and learning how naughty we humans really are.

Did you know that, according to the infidelity statistics, about 40 per cent of unmarried relationships and 25 per cent of marriages see at least one incident of infidelity? It has also been suggested that 70% of all Americans engage in some kind of affair sometime during their marital life. Both in 2018 and in 2019, men are more likely to cheat than women. According to recent data gathered from the General Social Survey, 20 per cent of the interviewed men and 13 per cent of women admitted they had sex with someone other than their spouse while married.[4]

This, coupled with the statistics that close to 50 per cent of marriages these days end in divorce, makes me seriously question whether it's realistic for us to expect our husbands to be all things for us. And if monogamy really is natural. Because, if it is, why are so many of us challenged by our "natural instincts" and straying from it?

I am sure we don't willingly want to go out of our way to hurt our life partners, break up our families, embarrass or hurt our children, or be looked down on and be shunned by wider society.

Why is infidelity in swinging or "open" relationships so taboo when so many of us are doing it behind closed doors?

A quarter of all of couples "sleeping away" makes it seem like a pretty common occurrence to me.

Sounds as if we are all puppies pissing on the carpet in the spare room hoping our humans don't catch us.

---

[4] Cacilda Jethá and Christopher Ryan, Sex At Dawn (United States: Harper, 2010).

Diary Entry 12

Being all of me

So, I had been trying to honour the guidance not to start any new projects and to just tune in and write.

Usually, I am reading and listening to a few books and podcasts at the same time about business and wealth, but all that does is fuel my logical brain and drown out my intuition as I look for answers "out there" instead of trusting the wisdom within. So, recently, I have been leaning more into music to help me raise my state and listening to content from spiritual leaders to help me surrender.

A journal prompt I heard this morning on my walk was: "What would it look like to be even more of me? To be *all* of me?"

I started to ponder and came up with these points:

- I would be more confident and certain in my journey.
- I would feel supported and trust instead of always wondering if I'm "doing" enough.
- I would stop looking on social media for other influencers who have what I want; I would stop comparing.

- I would spend less time in my social media feed and more time focused on writing, creating, being outdoors, blocking out time, and batching activities.
- I would tap more into my intuition, feeling magical, expecting miracles, feeling full, expansive, and grateful. I would be marvelled by the universe's wonder.
- I would spend more time connected to and conversing with my intuition and the universe, spirituality. I would transcribe that through teaching, coaching, and writing.

The next journal prompt asked me: "If I were already at my next level, hitting all my goals with ease, what would my schedule look like and what activities would fill my day?"

I started to map out my day:

6:30 a.m.: Get up, make myself a warm lemon water, snuggle up on my couch with Pumbaa and a candle, and start writing.

8:30 a.m.: Get out in the sunshine for a beach walk, listen to Personal Development or music (whatever I feel called to do that day), meditate, journal, and write my social media post for the day whilst feeling inspired and connected.

10:00 a.m.–noon: Break my fast with brunch, shower, get dressed, and feel refreshed and energised for group coaching or mentor calls.

12–2 p.m.: Check in with clients, reply to messages, empty my inboxes.

2–6 p.m.: Be available for life coaching calls, mentor calls, sales calls. In the white space between booked calls, go to the gym and enjoy a sauna session a few days a week.

6 p.m.: Put away my computer. Go for a dinner date with my husband, cook when I feel called to, or pay a chef to have our meals ready made so we can enjoy some quality time together or with friends and family.

9 p.m. Go to bed, read, and write in my gratitude journal (and make love!).

Next, I was prompted to journal: "Since I'm fully my next level *now*, the energy, emotions, feelings, that I feel and actions that I take are:"

- I will start honouring that schedule now.
- I will commit to journaling every night and being more intentional to connect with gratitude every single day.
- I will keep coming back to my affirmation "relinquish control, surrender to faith, and allow joy" throughout my day to anchor my intention, be in control of my energetic state, and remind myself I am on time.

Something that resonated with me this morning while I was listening to a spiritual leader was the idea that we don't have to do something to receive. Instead, flip it. We already have received, so what would we like to do?"

As a recovering human doing, I realised that, usually, we plan our days, our weeks, our years (heck, more like our entire lives) under the pretence that we do it in order to get something or achieve something in return. It might be a pay check, a goal, accolades, recognition, time off.

But what if I flipped it? Instead of doing something to receive, what if I looked around and realised I had already received.

I am blessed.

Extremely blessed.

I have my health. A husband and life partner who loves, respects, cares and challenges me. A cute little puppy I once dreamed of. A beautiful apartment filled with natural light, just like a picture I had glued on my vision board. I live free from war or poverty. I have an abundance of money which enables me to pay all my bills with gratitude and feel safe and secure. My immediate family are all alive and well. Time expands for me, and I get to spend it doing what I love instead of feeling restricted and suffocated in my old nine-to-five job. And I get to walk down to the beach every day.

So, I think it is fair to say I have received a wealth of blessings. Now I ask myself, what would I like to give?

When you come from that space; you get to ask yourself what would you love to give, contribute, or create out of choice, inspiration, flow, and alignment.

For me, it's another book.

It's a space.

It's a community.

It's resources.

It's a resource for women that can help them grow and be supported and take guided and inspired action. It's a place women can retreat to or seek out to feel expansive, liberated, supported, guided, magical, feminine yet fierce. Empowered. Independent yet also in perfect harmony and peace knowing that they are synchronising with something bigger than themselves.

It's funny. As I write this, the word *independent* feels flat or empty to me; once upon a time, it fuelled me.

I have always been independent myself. I've never needed or ever allowed myself to be in a position in which I needed someone or something. I have taken pride in the fact that, if I want something, I always get it or do it myself.

But it's as if the word has burnt itself out. It has no gas left in the tank. It's like a soldier tipping his hat off to me relieving himself of his duties, and I'm thanking him for his loyal service. He has been with me in the trenches and got me through so many battles. But this is where the road ends with us as comrades. It's as if the war is over and there is no need to fight or struggle anymore.

But without all the explosions and crawling through the muddy trenches, it's challenging to return to normality with ease, flow, and peace. It's challenging to think I no longer need independence as my armour.

Yes, independence got me to where I am today. It made me successful. It fuelled me for nearly a decade. But it can't carry me any longer.

Independence used to get me fired up and passionate (not only about my own journey but empowering other women with their finances and support to be independent), but it's no longer an energetic match for where I am or where I want to go.

I think I have finally understood what people mean when they say, "If you want to go fast, go alone. (Which I definitely have.) But if you want to go far, go together."

This rings true to me on so many levels right now.

I've noticed that, in my business, I have been unconsciously leaning into my team for support rather than leading myself. I have been trusting leaders in my business to rise up and do things that I had been doing for years. I am not coming up with all the answers. I have been relinquishing control and allowing other team members to contribute, innovate, and problem-solve to create resources.

I've noticed that I am letting go of my perfectionism, need to control, and need to double-check that everything is done to my standard. If the whole idea of this Surrender Project is to trust and allow things to be easy, I haven't felt the fire or the tenacity to keep pushing in my business or lead. So I've honoured that. Instead of pushing against the resistance, I am flowing with it and being so grateful for our collaborative business model.

No wonder 80 per cent of businesses fail in the first four years and so many business owners burn out and suffer adrenal fatigue.

If it wasn't for our collaborative business model within the network marketing profession, I don't think I would be able to move the needle by myself. If we want to go further, I am going to have to surrender, ask for help, accept help, and work as a team member.

I guess that's why we are here, isn't it?

This is where the Surrender Project was born.

Is it because I don't know where to go from here? I'm done trying to work it out, will, and force it myself. So I am surrendering myself to something bigger and trusting that wherever I am being guided to. I am not figuring it out alone. I am ready to listen.

Note: Since I'm focusing on fully being my next level *now* and pondering on my energy, emotions, and feelings as well as the actions I will take, I decided that the "next level of me" would not wait until I felt worthy of spending money on things I have always wanted to do for myself (like laser hair removal!) that I have always thought it was expensive. But since doing this little activity, I thought, *F#*k it! I have the money there in my "splurge" account. That is what it's meant for—to spend on me!* The "next level of me" wouldn't have to argue and convince herself she is worthy of spending her own pay check on grooming and beauty. Her "worthydometer" would be turned right up!

Besides, because of the pandemic, many businesses have been closed, and there hasn't been much to do; there haven't been many places to go. The money that I would have spent on non-pandemic weekend fun had been accumulating. It was sitting there. I had looked into laser treatments previously, but it never was the right time because the clinician always told me I would have to be out of the sun, and I wouldn't be able to tan. And if you know me, you know that is just not an option. Sunshine is my non-negotiable need. Usually, even in winter, we chase the sun and spend the cooler months in Europe or Bali. But all our travel plans had been cancelled for twelve months. It was winter. And I had the money sitting there.

So I booked myself in.

*F#*k!* Why does beauty have to be painful? First Botox now laser treatment. Women, what are we doing to ourselves? Don't get me wrong. I am doing this for me. I am sick of shaving, and I love the feeling of smooth, sexy legs when I glide into bed. But really? *Why* does it have to hurt this much?

I hope landing strips don't come back in fashion. I guess I'll keep my eye out for porn's latest pubic hair fashion!

Bye, pubic hair. Hello eight-year-old vagina.

Diary Entry 13

Finding my flow again

Is it possible to be in "flow" all the time?

And what does "flow" even feel like?

These were questions I was pondering this morning on my walk.

Because I have experienced flow in different periods of my personal and business life. I know it's like an energetic vortex we get to leverage. Kinda like in the movie *Finding Nemo* movie when the surfer-dude sea turtle, Crush, describes the EAC (East Australia Current) as the superhighway where turtles can hitch a free ride from one place to another.

But outside of Disney movies, flow is not a free ride. It costs us our courage, our faith, and our control. And before we're allowed on board, we have to leave our egos at the door.

For me it feels more like a wave.

A wave of energy.

A current of magic.

But when we're not in it, we feel as if we're behind the wave, pushing and trying to catch up with it, but no matter how much energy we exert, we're going against the current and not getting anywhere.

It feels as if there is an energetic block in our throat chakras.

But if we do the work, if we paddle ourselves out to make sure we're in position, we sit in the stillness, we tune into the universe's vibration, we surrender to the ocean's natural ebbs and flows and can feel the energy building, we lean in and trust the pull, the perfect wave comes.

Some call it luck, but you know that luck is just what happens when preparation meets opportunity.

It feels as if we've been preparing our whole lives for this.

All we need to do is take a few confident strides, back ourselves, and believe in something that others might not be able to see (yet), and we'll be riding the wave.

The energy starts to move through us, shifting from the block in our throats to beaming and pulsating out of our hearts.

We're able to leverage the power of alignment and of divine timing. We go far, but it's not hard work.

We soar with grace and ease as if we're being guided, fuelled, and supported by something bigger than us.

That's what flow feels like for me.

And to be honest, it feels as if I've been behind the wave for the last six months.

But this year, I have paddled outside of my comfort zone where most of us don't dare to swim. It's just been me and my thoughts. It's been lonely and vast. But I've been listening, tuning in, and leaning in.

I feel something building and shifting.

I think some people misinterpret flow. They describe it as something easy or a passive experience. Being in flow doesn't mean that we're not scared and you don't have moments of doubt. We just have to consciously keep reminding ourselves to surrender, and if we're going to go where we've never been before, understand that it's going to feel scary and probably not logical. Considering that we perceive, understand, and explain experiences by comparing them to past experiences, if we're going to experience something completely new, we won't be able to rely on our previous experiences to manage our expectations and make us feel comfortable.

This is uncharted territory.

It's only for the wild ones who dare to go where most won't.

Yes, flow feels good, but not good as in gluttony, as if we're sitting on our asses indulging in excessive amounts and being greedy. We still have to take inspired action even when it's uncomfortable to do so. And we take or trust what our souls need or desire, which won't be everything.

Our souls have unique footprints; they yearn for certain things. Everyone's does.

If only we allowed ourselves to enjoy the stillness and to listen and honour it, maybe more of us would find peace.

I've been honouring how the "next level" of me would show up and what her day would look like by spending two hours in the morning writing and journaling. I don't know why it took me so long to work it out, but this is where I can tap into flow: writing. It doesn't necessarily have to be for anyone else's eyes, but as soon as I commit to being quiet and tuning out all the noise, downloads come through.

I don't know what to call it. Inspiration? Intuition? Guidance? Clairaudience?

Whatever it is, I haven't felt it since I sat down to write my last book. And I have felt lost ever since.

As I sit down to write, I relinquish control. I have no idea what is going to come through me—how it will start or end. But I trust that whatever needs to come through will show up. And I will observe it without judgement.

With this Surrender Project, I have been trying to listen to what my unique soul footprint yearns for. What is it here to do? What is my soul work? Have I completed it? Or where do I go next?

This is what comes through:

> You're on a journey to unravel and undress layers of yourself that aren't you. This project isn't about becoming who you are; it's about unbecoming everything you aren't.

> With each layer you shed, each belief that you let go of that no longer serves you, you become magnetic. Your magnetic force field gets stronger, and you start to pull in people with ease and grace. These are people who love to work with you and love to pay you. They feel alignment with your message and, even though they never admit it or say it out loud, they recognise their truth when you speak yours.

> This calms them, and each time they breathe, they exhale a little deeper. As they slow down and feel safe, they start to tune into the natural universal laws and rhythms. They naturally want to expand and organically they share your work with their friends and family.

> Money is not an exchange for your "work." Your soul work is not something you do and people pay you for. You give energy, you open your heart and allow your light to shine upon others freely, unconditionally, and lovingly. Some beams of light escape into crevices that have been dark for a long time. You bring warmth, hope and faith.

> You share your teachings and energetic vibrations through resources both paid and free. And that energy

returns to you like a boomerang at the highest level you're vibrating at because people love it—not because they owe you it. That money isn't costing anyone anything; it's just universal energy flowing in and out.

This feels good.

And those who know me will recognize that, even though this is apparently my truth, this is not the way I usually talk. I am logical, and this all sounds a little woo-woo. That is probably why I have suppressed these messages and not shared them. I was afraid of sounding like a crazy person.

And despite feeling good, I find it hard to believe my path or next chapter can be this easy. Because that sounds like a dream.

Why can't it be easy?

I am supposed to be "un-becoming" and letting go of belief systems that no longer serve me, but which ones are they?

I think, if I am honest, I must admit that I carry guilt around business and abundance (and money) being easy when my parents have had to work so hard for so many years to try to create their abundance. Who am I to have it easy when I have seen them struggle? I am not a better person than they are. Why am I more deserving of that than they? Or anyone else for that matter?

If it could be easy, why is it hard for so many of us?

Okay. There is my logical brain trying to rationalise and justify.

I surrender.

If life and business are to be easy and flow with grace, I would spend my ideal mornings being free, expansive, in flow, writing, getting outside, walking my dog, getting in the sunshine, enjoying a coffee with a girlfriend (a new habit I have picked up, let me add, since starting this project—if decaf mochas count?), and listening to the sound of waves. Then I "work" from one to six in the afternoon. And by work, I mean be the light for women, holding space. Not coaching unless they come to me and want to invest and meet me at that energetic level. I am building and investing in my community, making sure they feel loved and enough and know how grateful I am to have them in my orbit. I have let go of resistance, and I lean into my systems, existing resources, and leadership.

In the afternoons, I leverage the energy of group calls. I help my team step into their light and leadership by mentoring and helping them with their first few calls and opening myself up for private soulmate coaching clients.

I had a breakthrough while I was pondering the beliefs that no longer were serving me. I realised that I hadn't actually worked hard to get to this point in my life or business. Yes, I have hustled, taken a lot of action, and achieved what most haven't, but it was by taking lots of inspired action and trusting that pull, that tug from my gut even when it was scary but which, at the time, felt aligned and in flow. The only reason I am feeling the way I am at the moment is that the thought of hustling again is no longer aligned. The next step or level or chapter (whatever you want to label it) is just continuing to take inspired action from here.

Not there.

And that inspired action might just look different.

It's not that I am stuck or stagnant or have hit an upper limit.

A tree doesn't have glass ceilings or upper limits. We are all just energy. We are made up of the same things as everything else in nature. Just think, we are all just growing. With the right environment and nourishment, you will continue to grow and expand. Naturally. With ease and grace. Not force.

It's a law of nature, so we need to stop restricting ourselves and putting limits on how things have to be and where we feel we should be and focus on nourishing our bodies and souls instead and just allowing ourselves to effortlessly flourish.

Well, then, I'm moving forward and letting go of beliefs that no longer serve me. I want to thank my fears and my independence.

I see you.

Thank you.

But I've got this.

I appreciate that you have got me this far. Fear and independence, you got me here, fuelled my work ethic. I understand why you helped me in those situations.

First you helped me have the courage and commitment to move away from home at eighteen to pursue my own dreams, pave my own way and future.

You encouraged me to travel the world so I could enjoy all of life's beauty and different cultures without having the regrets a lot of mums have later in life.

You fuelled me and drove me to create a business and residual income streams that ensure I will never need a man for security or safety and will be able to enjoy magical moments with my future kids without having to stress about work or missing them growing up.

You also gave me the drive and passion to pay that gift forward and create a space, a community, a container, and vehicle that enables so many other women to take control of their lives and futures so they can create that safety, security, and support for themselves too.

I appreciate you for stepping in.

We are safe now.

I see you.

I thank you.

I release you.

Now I choose some new beliefs.

I get to have it all on my terms—or something better.

Diary Entry 14

Breath work (and rejection)

Do I trust and believe in my bigger vision?

Are my needs taken care of today?

Okay, if I trust and believe and my needs are taken care of, what's my next aligned action?

These were some questions and journal prompts I picked up from a spiritual leader I have been listening to on my walks.

I was using them to help me lean into my intuition each morning to find guidance and stay on my path.

One of my goals that that I posted on my bathroom mirror this year was to explore and experience some more modalities in the alternative realm of medicine and wellness—reiki, energy healing, psychic or spiritual readings, kundalini, coca, or an ayahuasca ceremony.

Earlier this year, before the pandemic sent us all to our rooms for being naughty to think about what we had done to Mother Earth, I was in Bali with some of our closest friends. (I totally agree; we should all be sent to our rooms after seeing what we have done to Bali's beautiful oceans!) We wanted to do a breath-work session on our trip. However, the timing just didn't line up, so for my girlfriend's birthday, I surprised her over the weekend and organised a private class here in Australia that we could all attend together.

I don't know what I expected. I guess I am intrigued by the various levels of consciousness and psychology. And I love experiences, which is why I wanted to explore the different modalities.

Experiences are the only things we get to take with us to the grave, so I am always conscious of wanting to try new things and live a vibrant life of diversity, colours, cultures, emotions, and investing in experiences rather than things.

I tried to go into the breath-work class with no expectations. I planned to just surrender.

Which I felt I did.

I was calm. I went to a place where I just felt held.

There was no intuition. There were no messages, downloads, or visuals coming through. Just complete stillness, calmness, and confidence. I guess I felt some sort of acknowledgment that I've got this. The answers weren't in an experience or outside of myself. I just needed to trust myself and my gut without questioning, without the fear or doubt, and just know everything is on time and I am exactly where I need to be. This is the guidance or connection I am looking for. It's here within me.

After the class, the facilitator encouraged us to share, one by one, our internal experiences and what came up for us. There were four couples, so eight friends in total, and we all had such different experiences. Some tapped into a creative space, some cried, some had breakthroughs. Even my husband, who is a sceptic, seemed to tap into another realm of consciousness.

I would be lying if I said I wasn't just a little disappointed. I know I said I went into it with no expectations, so I don't think I was expecting fireworks or crazy earth-moving stuff, ground-breaking clarity, or visions. But something?

But I guess that was my return on my investment.

Sometimes we invest in things and don't get what we want. But we get what we need. I didn't get an answer or guidance, but I realised *that was* my guidance. I have the answers within.

So, I guess I did get what I paid for.

I had been following the breadcrumbs and leaning in when new opportunities came my way trusting the universe was deliberately placing them on my path for a reason. So instead of letting my ego or judgement get in the way, I surrendered.

Several months ago, I received an email from Griffith University Alumni requesting that I apply for an award. They were recognising alumni who had done and achieved amazing things since graduation. I had also been forwarded an application for the National Achievers Congress who were looking for women who had a message and mission they wanted to share from the stage.

I surrendered. Without judgement or ego, or the self-evaluation to decide if I was good enough or worthy, I filled out both applications without any emotional attachment.

I have always done this though. When opportunities arise, I have always backed myself and at least applied. This isn't so much spiritual for me; it's more logical. I always go the extra mile because it's less crowded. I feel as though so many people get in their own way and in their own heads and put everyone else on a pedestal and themselves in the pit. They overestimate what everyone else is doing and underestimate what they could do if they just committed to showing up for themselves consistently.

I didn't apply because I thought myself amazing or better than anyone else. I was motivated more by a logical (and statistical) understanding that most people feel they are shit so they don't apply. That gave me better odds. I had a better chance of winning or receiving the position merely just by putting myself forward to be considered rather than sitting back with the masses who spend a lot of time talking about what they don't want instead of taking opportunities and risks to create something they do want.

What do they say? You've got to buy a ticket to win the lottery?

I have always done this. And some of the best blessings of my life have come from saying yes and exploring new opportunities instead of letting fear of rejection or failure keep me stagnant in the same place whinging and moaning about how I wasn't where I wanted to be.

Saying yes, putting myself out there, and just trying or applying led to my scholarship; moving to the Gold Coast; getting a second scholarship and moving to Hawaii; getting a graduate position in child protection; starting a network marketing business, which totally transformed my life and lifestyle; talking on stages around the world in front of thousands of people; and writing and publishing books.

I try to follow the breadcrumbs and test what doors will open for me and just trust that the ones that don't weren't meant for me instead of berating myself and turning the closed doors into self-fulfilling negative prophecies and confirmation of my original belief of how shit I am.

For that reason, I feel that most people just think successful people don't get rejection. But it's just because we don't take rejection personally or ruminate over it and allow it to keep us from moving forward.

So I am kind of glad that, this week, I got two rejection emails pretty much a day apart. This way you can see the process that most people don't get to see behind the scenes because rejection usually isn't something documented, announced from the rooftop, or shared publicly.

But it's part of the journey.

So, if those doors weren't meant for me, I am excited to see what door opens next.

I'm still here.

Surrendering.

I'm still being curious, being playful, and following the breadcrumbs. It's like a game of snakes and ladders. I am being careful not to be fooled and slip backwards by my ego or fear. But I'm also on the lookout for the ladder—that next step to the next level.

Diary Entry 15

The next level

WHAT IS THE NEXT LEVEL?

Why do we continuously need to be striving, achieving, and pursuing the next thing?

Why can't I stay still? Why do I have to keep growing?

Is it part of society that has pressured us to feel that we always have to be constantly doing? Or is part of our nature that we are always going to be growing—like a plant?

Life is actually really good. Why can't I be happy here? Why do I need to be striving or wanting to achieve or have more?

Well ...

I am torn between science and spirituality. Torn between what is logical and makes sense, and what is intuitive and feels good. In my previous book, *Life Above Zero*, I explain that science has discovered that happiness is found within the experience of flow, which can be found only when we stretch ourselves and our capabilities. I guess this is where the element of growth comes from. Because if we stand still with no goals and nothing to strive for, we become bored, restless, and start to feel as if we have no purpose.

But then, we hear about the pursuit of happiness and that happiness is habitual. We learn that when we have more, our level of happiness adapts and increases our need to maintain or increase that level of fulfilment or satisfaction. This is why happiness always seems to be out of reach. We turn what we have into enough by consciously choosing to practise gratitude.

I guess this new woo-woo term *manifestation* that seems to be everywhere these days merges both these theories together. It meets these ideologies in the middle and acknowledges that both are true.

It's a strategic dance—being so grateful for what we have and allowing those feelings to embody our beings and raise our energetic vibrations. From that place of abundance, we attract more abundance and transcend to that next level or achieve that goal we have been wanting—without force, hustle, or desperation.

Kinda like men who have mastered the art of flirting. They make themselves desirable and play hard to get as if they don't care or need you because they have an abundance of women's numbers saved in their phones to dial for late-night booty calls. They have no attachment, and this inevitably attracts even more women to them like flies.

Manifestation is grounded in quantum physics, the law of energy. It seems to be the new high-ticket item that coaches themselves invest in when all logical business strategies fail. These light workers around the world claim they are part of the movement that is raising the world's consciousness.

Do I believe in it?

I don't know.

It seems that all these crazy people have decided overnight that, without any study, schooling, or qualifications, they are going to start charging people ten to thirty thousand dollars to help them believe in magic again. And people pay them believing that these people are magic themselves and have a secret they don't know. Is it because these light workers went from making zero to $300,000 in twelve months?

I can't help but feel that the coaching world has turned into a pyramid scheme: coaches just working with coaches and coaching them to raise their prices to work with more coaches. Then a coach raises her price and invests in another coach who charges more and encourages her to charge more so she can continue just working with coaches and helping them charge more.

Do these light workers at the top of the pyramid have a secret? Are they the crazy ones setting their services at ridiculously high prices that aren't logical so we believe it's a magical, spiritual thing?

Or are we the crazy ones willing to pay what they charge, thinking that, if they have achieved that level of self-worth, they must have something we don't have as we continue to look for answers, fulfilment, and success outside of ourselves?

I don't know.

They say money is just energy, so maybe this comes back to my own self-limiting beliefs about having to work hard to create it, and this just contradicts my most dominating belief system. This is probably why I have trouble wrapping my head around it.

I don't have the answers. I don't think there is one reality, or right or wrong. It is all subjective. But I am trying to make sense of my reality by thinking out loud in this Surrender Project.

Several years ago, I read *The Big Leap: Conquer Your Hidden Fear and Take Life to the Next Level* by Gay Hendricks. Hendricks writes about all of us having our own upper limits. And, as humans, we feel guilty when things are going well or when we feel good (and we doubt it will last long), so we self-sabotage and unconsciously cause ourselves to suffer.

I couldn't help but wonder if this was my big leap.

Was I being faced with my own upper limit? Do I feel guilty that life is good, business is easy, and time expands, so now I have created a scenario in my head that I need to suffer?

Is the Surrender Project my own self-inflicted version of suffering? Do I doubt that I am deserving of such a good life? Do I doubt that it will last so I've created a scenario in which something is wrong or needs to be fixed instead of allowing myself to enjoy this space?

Maybe.

I have been pulling angel cards tarot every morning to help me tap into my intuition. I have kept pulling this card known as "conflict resolution." It seems to be a regular occurrence no matter how many times I shuffle the deck.

Angel Archangel guides:

> This is the time for realising that when you see two polarities playing out it is always forming a whole picture. If we are balanced to begin with, then we don't need to play at the polarity outside of ourselves. When you can see the lesson within a conflict, you can then balance the issue within yourself and thereby release the need to play out the issue which releases others from having to play out their role in a conflict too.[5]

I am not sure what this message means, but as I have pondered on it and tried to make sense of it, I have realised that I need to stop identifying and labelling myself as a human doing. By allowing myself to be dominated by my masculine energy, I am creating the need for the polar opposite—the feminine energy of being.

The more I reinforce my reality and identity—consciously through words spoken and written and unconsciously through thought—I

[5] Carisa Mellado, Ask An Angel (Victoria, Australia: Blue Angel Publishing, 2012).

co-create the conflict that a Surrender Project is necessary if I am to solve my imbalance and resolve my inner conflicts and external challenges.

Instead, I am whole.

I am both feminine and masculine.

I do, and I also be. One is not at the expense of the other. They are just different sides of the same coin.

I have always believed and understood that we create our reality and speak it into existence through our words and thoughts. So, going forward, I've made a commitment to myself to no longer speak or identify as a human doing who is challenged. Because all that does is just reinforce my belief, my identity, and my internal struggle.

Instead, I am choosing to affirm that life is magical. Miracles happen every day. I am not in control. I am just focusing on being present, taking inspired action when opportunities present themselves and cross my path, and committing to enjoying the journey.

And what about the next level?

I am not convinced it exists.

I am reminded of one of my favourite stories, the fisherman and businessman:

> There was once a businessman who was sitting by the beach in a small village. As he sat, he saw a fisherman rowing a small boat towards him. He noticed the fisherman had caught quite a few big fish. The businessman was impressed and asked the fisherman, "How long does it take you to catch so many fish?"
>
> The fisherman replied, "Oh, just a short while."
>
> "Then why don't you stay longer at sea and catch even more?" The businessman was astonished.

"This is enough to feed my entire family," the fisherman said.

The businessman then asked, "So, what do you do for the rest of the day?"

The fisherman replied, "Well, I usually wake up early in the morning, go out to sea and catch a few fish, then go back and play with my kids. In the afternoon, I take a nap with my wife. When evening comes, I join my buddies in the village for a drink. We play guitar, sing, and dance throughout the night."

The businessman offered a suggestion to the fisherman. "I have a PhD in business management. I could help you to become a more successful person. From now on, you should spend more time at sea catching as many fish as possible. When you have saved enough money, you could buy a bigger boat and catch even more fish. Soon you would be able to afford to buy more boats, set up your own company, your own production plant for canned food, and a distribution network. By then, you will have moved out of this village and to the city, where you can set up headquarters to manage your other branches."

The fisherman asked, "And after that?"

The businessman laughed heartily. "After that, you can live like a king in your own house, and when the time is right, you can go public and float your shares in the stock exchange. You will be rich!"

The fisherman asked, "And after that?"

The businessman said, "After that, you can finally retire. You can move to a house by the fishing village, wake up early in the morning, catch a few fish, then return home to play with your kids, have a nice afternoon nap with your wife, and when evening comes, you can join your buddies for a drink, play the guitar, sing, and dance throughout the night!"

The fisherman was puzzled, "Isn't that what I am doing now?"

I am not convinced that the answer is found by working more, creating more money, or receiving more accolades.

Yes, money to a certain extent provides a level of happiness and safety when you are able to meet yours and your family's immediate needs like food, water, shelter, clothes, schooling, and so forth.

Studies have shown that, once a person attains a yearly income of $80,000, additional income doesn't seem to correlate with higher happiness ratings. So, once you have navigated the next level (think of a game of Mario Kart) and you start making more than $80,000 a year, your happiness is found in the small stuff. Don't fall into the trap of believing you'll find happiness chasing the big stuff.

On that note, I have spent the last couple of hours of my Wednesday morning writing. I slept in and enjoyed cuddles with my husband (and missed my gym class). And now I am going to play with my dog.

Life *is* magical. Miracles happen every day. I am not in control. I am just focusing on being present, taking inspired action when opportunities present themselves and cross my path, and committing to *enjoying* the journey.

Diary Entry 16

OKAY, SO AS YOU KNOW, I HAVE BEEN READING ABOUT THE EVOLUTION of sexuality and gender psychology just for fun. And if I am honest, I have to admit that something that I keep coming back to is the concept of monogamy.

The more I read about it, the more I realise it's just a system that was constructed. A bunch of humans got together hundreds of years ago and decided that they would have private properties and no longer live in tribes where childbearing and resources were shared; however, each man would need to own his women. Because, if men were going to be out ploughing the fields, they would need their women in the home. And because there would be only finite resources with fewer hands to do the work, they wouldn't want to spend their limited resources on kids that weren't theirs. Men who owned their women would know the kids their women give birth to were theirs; they would not be left paying for someone else's offspring.

Why did the majority of us buy into that system?

Yes, it makes sense economically.

But emotionally, spiritually, sexually, biologically, realistically?

Before this, for thousands of years all around the world in different cultures, people loved (and f#*ked) each other freely without guilt, shame, or having to lie and hurt their loved ones over it.

Because it was natural.

It *is* natural.

It may not already be apparent to you, but I don't think the system we have created for ourselves and bought into is working. One in two marriages end in divorce. That seems like a pretty big failure rate for something that is supposed to come naturally to us.

Monogamy and marriage are social constructs. We've made them up, and the system is so ingrained into most of us that we feel an overwhelming sense of shame for just being ourselves and enjoying what feels good.

This drives many of us to question if there is something wrong with us. We sneak around, cheat, suppress sexual fantasies, hide porn addictions, and break up families and homes. It seems as if humans in the Western world have created our own upper limit when it comes to monogamy and inflicting suffering on ourselves.

People turn to cute little penguins to restore their faith and find reassurance that monogamy is doable. After all, these cute little things devote their lives to each other. That's a lot of weight and responsibility for a poor little penguin to carry considering none of the other animals are being relied on to restore the human faith. They get to have orgies all day.

But I feel that only a piece of this story has told to justify our biases and confirm our narrative to help us find comfort in our choices. Because, yes, penguins are monogamous, but that just means that a male breeds with one female during a mating season. After the childrearing duties are over, they move on and f#*k someone else. They are just mindful that promiscuity could affect their ability to focus on loving and providing their baby with what they need to survive. So, for a brief period of time, they selflessly put their sexual urges aside and put their kids before their dicks.

How considerate of them.

Maybe we humans could learn a thing or two?

But don't get it twisted. Penguins enjoy the novelty, excitement, and variety that comes with having sex with many different penguins. They just practise serial monogamy whilst looking after kids. Because, let's be honest, kids are needy; they need your attention (and sex can take up a lot of brain space).

Another belief system I've become increasingly aware of over the last four years since starting my own network marketing business is the belief that we need to, should, are expected to work nine to five, Monday to Friday. Once again, who got around a table and decided that was a good idea and dictated that is how the rest of us had to spend our time for fifty years of our lives (in hope that we are still around and healthy enough to enjoy retirement afterwards)?

I don't remember being asked to vote on that.

But somewhere along the way, the Western world bought into that concept.

It's taken me years to dislodge that belief system. And, as you can see, it's so deeply indoctrinated in my mind after twenty years of traditional schooling, I am still actively working every day to change it.

I am not a rebel or an anarchist going against the system or going against the grain. I'm actually something opposite. I have just stopped buying into the brainwashing. I've stopped fighting the resistance of trying to live in a way that doesn't feel natural. I don't believe we are here to work until we die. I am just working out ways (such as network marketing) to be and to enjoy life the way we are all intended to.

I am uncovering layers (and years) of conditioned belief systems that no longer serve me or align with the way I want to live. It's not as if I am becoming something or someone different; I am just un-becoming everything we aren't and have been brainwashed to believe we are.

For the last four years, I have been consciously rewiring how I choose to think about work, life, and the way I create money (which is just the resources we need to enjoy life). At the rate Australia is printing money right now to deal with the pandemic and the global financial crises, money won't have the value we have perceived it to have, and we'll probably go back to trading milk for eggs anyway.

Because money, too, is a social construct.

It's not real.

We made it up.

A $20 note is only worth $20 because we all agree it is. What if we all just looked at it and realised it's a piece of freaking paper? And what if we questioned if it's really worth trading an hour of our precious lives for a piece of paper?

We have all been indoctrinated, domesticated, encultured, and brainwashed into a following book of laws. Everything is made up by us—by society, culture, religion, and language. We got together over the years and made up certain things. Then, as a group, we decided those things are true and we continue to hold that those beliefs have truth as long as we agree that they still exist.

These laws may be what many people have chosen as their truth, but it's not the infinite universal truth, and I am still working out what money and marriage mean to me. Obviously, my husband and I have open discussions about this because that was a promise we made to each other, but what that partnership looks like is up to us.

I don't want to buy into those societal norms and be one of the two marriages that end in divorce.

I don't agree with other people's ideas of how my days should look or what I need to do to deserve or attract money to enjoy my life.

It's all just a social construct. It's not nature. It's nurture, and so many of the "rules" we live by are made up.

So, as easy as it is to make something up, I'm creating something different.

I laugh when people refer to my colleagues and I working in the network marketing profession as a cult. We are not the crazy ones. Choosing to work yourself into the ground, trading your time for a piece of paper—that sounds like the definition of crazy to me!

We are just living, loving, working, and playing the way "god" intended us to, sharing services and products we are passionate about and would organically share even if we weren't getting paid to.

I shouldn't feel guilty for slowing down and not working fifty hours a week. I'm not doing anything wrong; I am just surrendering and allowing my life to be the way life was lived thousands of years ago before humanity intervened and thought they knew better.

When it comes to marriage, why have we been groomed to believe love is a zero-sum equation? Why is it so easy to believe and experience that a mother's love isn't a zero-sum proposition? She can love all her children equally. But when it comes to sexual love, that is a finite resource.

When it comes to money, why do we feel guilty for having more when there are people who don't have enough? Money isn't a zero-sum equation. Money too is an infinite resource. Just because some have more doesn't mean there is less for someone else.

We experience feelings of scarcity and jealousy only when we lack trust.

You don't order nachos off the menu and wonder if you're worthy to have them or worry that they might not show up in front of you. You order nachos and they show up because you have no energetic charge around it. They arrive because you trust.

Well, listen up.

I am ordering a big juicy life of love, passion, hot sex, trust, magic, miracles, flow, sunshine, and family off the menu.

Why do we govern, judge, restrain, and discipline everything that feels good?

I want to challenge your beliefs. Now, this may trigger you, but that's the point. Hear me out.

If I wanted to have sex with a hot random man I meet out on the weekend, why don't I? Because, firstly, I wouldn't want to hurt or deceive my husband because I love him, care for him, and respect him. Secondly, I don't want to be shunned and judged by society. But I can promise you (I've learned during lots of chats with my girlfriends) that most of us want to. My decision is not a question of nature; it's nurture. The instinct is there. It's our loyalty and society that says that's not okay.

But what if your partner knew what you wanted and you talked about it openly and agreed it was okay, it fit within your meaning of marriage? And what if society woke up and realised they are living by a made-up moral code that goes against what's real in our innate nature? Would they be so quick to judge, condemn, and villainise?

What if I wanted to swim and sit in the sun today instead of work? Well, when I was working in corporate, I would have had to lie and fake a sickie or probably lose my job. If I was honest, I would say I'd rather enjoy my time outside today.

What if we all just did more of what felt good and lived more by our natural instinctual codes rather than our social nurtured ones?

Would we all just turn into gluttons or lazy pieces of self-absorbed shit? Would we all just binge on our ecstasies?

Because, if we were honest with ourselves, we would have to admit that, being intuitive and following and acting on what felt good, we would stop at a point because our bodies would communicate with us that we were full, satisfied, or tired.

I think about this even in terms of retirement. Even if we didn't have to work, we would still find a way to contribute to society and create or be of service because it feels good. We all need something to do.

What if we all just did more of what feels good rather than doing what society has groomed us to feel like we should or have to do?

Would we find ourselves in more loving, trusting, open relationships? Would we lead more fulfilling and soul-aligned careers and businesses?

What if?

I am on a quest to find out.

Note: My mum and dad will be coming for an extended visit tomorrow, and in the spirit of my Surrender Project, I am going to test this out. Over the next two weeks I'll be checking in with my private coaching clients and women I am mentoring in business. I'll do this between long morning walks, reading, writing, massages, cocktails, and soul chats with my parents.

I made a little challenge with myself that I would not create boundaries that would segregate work time from holiday time. I don't want them to be separate. I want to get paid to live life; my full-time job is just sharing what I am passionate about and creating what I enjoy.

Up to this point, I have created freedom, but within certain rules: No work on weekends. Start work at 9:00 a.m. No work after 6:00 p.m.

But, as I said earlier, I am working on creating new belief systems. Actually, it's more like shedding them and returning to old ones like the ones early humans had when they lived in tribes. Work, leisure, learning and teaching, nature, and family time were scattered throughout the day without rigid structure or rules.

Who made the rules we follow anyway? Why do so many of us feel pressured to abide by them?

I fill up my cup. I enjoy time in nature with family members and friends. I slow down to eat my food and enjoy a siesta during the day.

I'm a vessel for light and connect on a soul level with whomever the universe puts on my path.

I trust.

I create when I'm inspired and in flow, and I rest when I'm called to. Without the guilt.

Am I crazy? Or did our society and culture make us crazy?

When did we start believing that we had to work a certain number of hours to make a certain amount of money, to reach a certain level of success, to deserve a break?

I know a lot of hard workers who aren't rich but do suffer from adrenal fatigue, obesity, and heart problems. I don't believe hard work is going to get you where you want to go. Clarity, alignment, a grateful heart, and consistent inspired action will.

My business is just an extension of me and an expression of all that I am—sunshine, beach, travel, family, psychology and mindset, holistic health, self-love and compassion, women empowerment, business and wealth creation. So, if my staycation is just me encouraging myself to lean more into what feels good, well, I might just end up working after all!

Diary Entry 17

Moon magic

IN THE SPIRIT OF SURRENDERING AND LEANING INTO MY FEMININE AND spirituality this year, I have read a lot of books that have made me aware of how cyclical we women are and how unrealistic it is for people to expect us to work like men, and be on the go, producing, achieving, and doing all the time.

Our bodies and energies move through seasons, and if you follow your hormones with your menstrual cycle or even the lunar cycle, you can find more intuitive ways to work and rest whilst still getting it all done.

My girlfriend and business bestie, Chani Thompson, has been tracking the moon for years. It's her jam and zone of genius! I was talking to her about my challenges with slowing down and also some of my doubts (or more like curiosities) around marriage and what makes a successful one in the twenty-first century.

We are both successful businesswomen ourselves, fiercely independent and passionate about empowering women with health, wealth, and personal development. We are very conscious of the lives we are creating for ourselves and the relationships we choose to cultivate.

We were talking about our mentors, our parents, and marriages that inspire us that we would want to emulate. Of course, the era we grew up in is different from the one our mothers grew up in. It's different because women these days have more power, choices, and opportunities, but it's challenging because now we are expected to be career women, business owners, wives, mums, homemakers, good friends, good daughters, good sisters.

How do these roles affect what we expect or tolerate in marriage if we are now doing more than we ever have before?

What does it mean in life partnerships when we are expected to lean more into our masculine side when it comes to money, running the household, romance, respect, our libido, and sex?

It was the full moon with the lunar eclipse in Capricorn. Don't ask me what that means because I have no idea! But Chani explained that these moments are opportunities to delve into our emotional self-triggering inner and emotional events that usually last six months. Where the eclipse is happening in your natal chart will determine what your inner reflections and lessons will be for the rest of the year.

Usually, people see a lunar eclipse as a time of resistance because usually what comes up for us isn't exactly what we want to dive into. But she encouraged me to not resist and see this time as a gift to make peace with whatever is being reflected to me. I should use this as an opportunity for growth and evolution.

Chani told me, "Lunar eclipses can be a perfect time to heal intense emotions. By opening ourselves up and going deep, we can tap into a state of self-actualisation and fulfilment that is rare to come by."

Chani helped me read my birth chart to see what was coming up for me with this eclipse that I would be leaning into and learning about for the rest of the year.

I figured why not? With this Surrender Project, I have leaned more into meditation, reiki, kinesiology and energy work, psychic readings, journaling and writing again, sex, breath work, angel cards, mindfulness, and marijuana. Let's give moon magic a go!

Apparently, this lunar eclipse was happening for me on the cusp of my seventh and eighth house.

> The seventh house rules relationships and marriage. It reveals our shadow selves and ideal partners. Many planets in the seventh house indicate an emphasis on relationships, over-identifying with others, and co-dependence. Ironically, this house also indicates open enemies. The signs and planets that fall into the seventh house show how we relate to relationships and marriage.

Huh, I thought to myself.

> The eighth house is the house of death, sex, birth, and psychology. Many planets here indicate the push toward deep inner work and transformation. Perhaps these natives would be therapists, shamans, hospice workers or doulas. Sexuality is emphasised as well as investigation and digging into the hidden aspects of the human experience. The planets and signs that fall into the eighth house indicate foremost how we relate to sexual intimacy.

Mmmm this moon magic is on point! Or is everyone questioning marriage and sex right now? Or is that personal to just my experience?

Being a Scorpio, I have always been a sexual and passionate person, but I have never thought more about men, sexuality, and marriage than I have this year since our wedding and making that lifetime commitment myself.

This year has propelled me into a world of books, podcasts, conversations, and discussions, and to be honest, I must reveal that I wish I didn't know what I know now because I can never unknow it or go back to my previous way of existence. I felt angry and annoyed that the feelings, thoughts, questions, information, and education I have stumbled across this year wasn't made aware to me before I made a vow to my best friend so I could have had those discussions with him then rather than now.

Don't get me wrong. My experience has inspired a lot of interesting conversations over dinner together and probably brought us closer together. But it probably would have made sense to discuss marriage *before* marriage! But as I was saying, I didn't have these thoughts or questions back then. I guess that is what marriage is. Continuing to evolve individually and commit to growing and learning together as you reintroduce new parts of yourself to the person you've chosen and committed to sharing this life with.

Was this experience normal and just like a rite of passage or a developmental stage women hit as we embark on our thirties and before starting a family?

Was it all the extra time the pandemic forced upon us during isolation that had sent me crazy?

Was it the lunar eclipse?

I don't know. But either way, I had questions.

What is even crazier is that, the next day, I was pulling my angel card as part of my morning routine and ritual, and I pulled the sexuality card. I have had this deck for twelve months, and I've pulled a card on most days, but I had never pulled this card or read it before. So I was curious to hear what it had to say:

> Sexuality is the physical expression of our soul's essence.
> Our sexual energy brings us to life. It puts a spark in
> our eyes, a kick in our step and a sway in our hips. It is

through our senses that we develop "sensitivity" on all levels. Through touch, sight, sound, smell and taste we awaken to the richness in life. It is through pleasure that we celebrate life and through ecstasy that we experience oneness with divinity and nature of the divine.

This may be a time for you to begin exploring and becoming sensitive to your physical self. Have you been honouring your body and sexuality as sacred? Does your physical being reflect and express your spiritual being? Do you allow yourself to feel sensitive and awake inside your body? Do you feel free to express yourself psychically and sexually?

This is a time for reflecting on these questions and bringing balance to this area of your life. If you have a relationship that needs healing in this area or you are wanting to bring in a new partner, you must first heal and balance these things within yourself. Others will only ever reflect the true and often hidden feelings you have about yourself.

Therefore, this is the time to love yourself, explore your sensuality, become sensitive, honour your body as sacred and enjoy your sexuality.[6]

Instead of trying to find the answers or work out what this guidance meant, I just let this sink in. I surrendered and promised myself I would lean into my vulnerability and see where this quest takes me as I continue to read and learn about gender psychology and sexuality for fun in my free time.

---

[6] Carisa Mellado, Ask An Angel (Victoria, Australia: Blue Angel Publishing, 2012).

Note: A life and business update. I did it!

My parents came to visit this week, and as I mentioned in my last diary entry, I had committed to no boundaries. There would be no "work" hours. I was present with my family, enjoying two-hour walks every day with mum, enjoyed an afternoon drink with my dad, and watched the sunset.

I created when I felt inspired to. I replied to messages and hopped on calls when I was excited to. And I did work tasks when it felt good to do them.

And what's even crazier is that I got more done in less time!

Naturally, every day I found myself wanting to sit down at my computer for a couple of hours, and surprisingly, I finished all the important stuff I needed to get done—the stuff that actually moves the needle in my business—in two hours! I guess it's true that 20 per cent of our input accounts for 80 per cent of our output. The rest is just fluff and not essential! (If you haven't already, check out the 80:20 rule.)

I had the biggest week in my business ever. I attracted the most team and clients, and I did it organically. I felt the most joy, expansion, and gratitude in business than I had in a long time. It wasn't forced, pushed, or willed. I showed up because I wanted to, not because I had to.

Downtime isn't wasted time.

Self-love isn't selfish; it's essential for serving others and having more impact.

You can do less and achieve more.

Okay, so now I get it and have experienced it. Can I now believe it?

I am going to remind myself about this and try to consciously honour it as I move forward.

Diary Entry 18

Would I date me?

THIS YEAR I AM UNRAVELLING A LOT OF LAYERS AND QUESTIONING A LOT of my truths or what I once used to believe to be true about a lot of things. Because there is really no one truth. The world isn't black or white. We get to choose our truths, and most times we construct them to serve our narratives.

Psychology has backed this up, and I discuss observer and attention biases in my book *Life Above Zero*.

But what I love most about this is that we can change our truths (and the way we look at the world) if we are conscious enough to be aware of our beliefs and have the desire to change them and are willing to do the inner work to rewrite them.

Business really is the most spiritual journey you will ever go on. The amount of personal development and mentorship I have unlocked since saying yes to the Juice Plus company five years ago, has meant I have always had the support and resources to facilitate my level ups. Year after year, I continue to grow, evolve, and learn more about myself and how to make the most out of this short human experience we are gifted with.

Although just as we say to the thousands of women we mentor in business, another level another devil. As soon as you break through to a new level of abundance, income, or leadership, you will be faced with a new self-limiting belief you need to dismantle in order to transcend again.

The road isn't linear and definitely isn't always comfortable. But if you're brave enough to lean into it, it's meaningful, and that's what many of us are looking for and are devoid of it. Yet so many people try to avoid pain, discomfort, and suffering without realising that, from these experiences, we derive purpose and meaning.

The last four years in my business has looked like a lot of inspired action, moving, and shaking, accolades, achievements, and creating content. This year (along with most of us in 2020 with the pandemic) I have been doing a lot of resting and turning inward.

Obviously, this is where the Surrender Project sprang from. For part of this year, I have been consuming more spiritual leaders' content as opposed to business strategists' content, and this was also a shift in focus within this Surrender Project.

A lot of spiritual leaders talk about money. And until I embarked on business, the subject of money was taboo. It was a matter of fact; it was a resource we needed to buy the essentials. But that's about it. There is not much more to talk about. You work for an hour. You get your wage. You exchange that for food, clothes, shelter, electricity, and whatever.

There were few open conversations about wealth creation and money. These subjects were not taught at school, university, or at home.

No wonder so many people struggle with their money. It's sad because it's the one thing we all need in the twenty-first century so we can survive and enjoy a higher quality of life.

I have done a lot of work on my money story and my relationship with money since embarking on business, and this year I leaned more into my spiritual relationship with money, which would sound kinda crazy to the Lauren of five years ago.

How can you even have a relationship with money?

But at its core, money is just energy manifested in physical form. Its value is whatever we believe it to be. It's infinite. Just like the sun, it's abundant AF.

The majority of us have scarcity mindsets. We have "truths" and limiting beliefs around the circulation of money.

Any of these thoughts or beliefs sound familiar?

- Money doesn't grow on trees.
- Time is money.
- You've got to work hard for your money.
- The rich get richer while the poor get poorer.
- Money in, money out.
- Easy come, easy go.
- There is more to life than money.
- Money doesn't bring you happiness.
- The love of money is the root of all evil.

A great book that helped me explore and bust through these concepts is *The Abundance Code: How to Bust the 7 Money Myths for a Rich Life Now* by Julie Cairns. Earlier in my business journey, I actually wrote a blog on some of the pivotal books that helped me change my relationship with money. Man, I have come a long way, but I still have to catch myself and continue to deconstruct beliefs that no longer serve me as I navigate my own journey.

In a podcast I was listening to the other week, a spiritual leader encouraged listeners to personify money so we could actually explore our spiritual relationship with it. So, we should think about money as if it were a person we wanted to date and ponder the following questions:

- Do you talk shit about your lover (money) when he isn't there?
- Do you trust him? Do you have faith that he will show up for you? (In other words, when you spend your money, do you trust that it's going to come back to you?)
- Are you clingy with your lover? Do you give him the space to love you back? Or are you insecure and need to control and restrain him to make sure he still loves you? (In other words, do you give your money away freely?)
- Do you come across desperate to your lover and have no self-worth? Do you chase him around like a lost puppy? (In other words, would you do anything for money even if you do not see it as a fair exchange for your time, expertise, or joy?)
- What kind of person would money be attracted to if it were a person?

I don't know about you, but I think of these words when I think about money: abundant, giving, expansive, trusting, and a high level of self-worth.

I started to wonder: If I were money, would I date me?

I have really been loving a few of the spiritual leaders I have been leaning into and have been inspired and excited to invest and work with them. I think all business owners should have some form of support—a mentor or a coach—to hold space for them and to help them navigate their way to their next level and get clarity as well as emotional support. We carry a lot of weight ourselves as that person for our employees and team. But something in me has been encouraging me to wait and lean into my own truth before drowning it out with more noise and someone else's truths and beliefs.

My intuition (which I am getting so much better at listening to and honouring even when it doesn't make sense and isn't comfortable) is telling me to explore my own thoughts and feelings and to turn inwards to find the answers instead of seeking them externally.

If I drown out the noise, meditate, and put my hands on my heart to connect, my inner wisdom tells me those courses and coaches will be amazing and they are for me. Just not yet. I have got more to uncover alone before I get help to take me further.

My inner wisdom keeps tugging me (and giving me a stern talking to, if I am honest) reminding me that I am still not listening and tuning in. (She's right.) I love reading and writing, but I still am not meditating and "being" regularly.

I need to listen to myself instead of others. I need to meditate and go deeper. I need to journal my dreams and tap into my psychic abilities. I have been told numerous times by healers and psychics that I have that ability. I just don't slow down enough to be able to tap into it.

I think we're all like that.

When wisdom comes through, it's quiet and calm. It's a different voice to that of my ego or even my conscious thoughts.

I get downloads only when I am still and connected—connected to my breath, connected to love, and connected, as one, with nature and humanity as a whole.

When my intuition and guidance come through, it's as if I am receiving a communication from a third person (it's not me). This third entity cradles my heart and makes me feel warm, supported, held, and guided as it whispers in my ear. (Sounds creepy as I write it, but I actually never feel safer than in those moments.)

I am not sure if it's clairaudient or clairsentience, but the messages always come through with either words or energies.

The messages are soft, and sometimes can get drowned out by my ego telling me they are crazy because they are not always logical or comfortable. But yet it always feels aligned.

I am still trying to master the art of letting her speak more often instead of filling the silence in my life with learning, podcasts, books, webinars, trainings, and courses.

It's a slow process, but I can't help but think that, if more of us would try to focus on our internal wisdom and intuition rather than external validation and opinions, we would all be a lot happier and less overwhelmed.

Diary Entry 19

Asking for a sign

I AM SPIRITUAL, BUT I GUESS I STILL TOY AND TEST MY FAITH EVERY NOW and then.

In the spiritual manifestation world, so many leaders have said we can ask for support from the universe or ask our spirit guides to send us a sign to communicate with us and especially to help us know we're on the right path.

Over the last few years, I have tested this, and I've definitely received messages that seem way too serendipitous to just be coincidental.

A few years ago, I was seeing the number eleven everywhere. But the academic researcher and realist in me downgraded the phenomenon: "Of course you are, Lauren. You've activated your observer and confirmation bias. Now you're looking for them, and you've primed your brain to filter them, so it makes sense you are now seeing them everywhere."

But it was getting a little freaky.

One night I was lying in bed. My husband had gone out for some beers with his mates. I woke up to music blaring in the middle of the night. I jumped out of bed to yell at him, assuming he had come home after a few too many drinks to kick on at our house. But there was no one in our apartment; my music had turned on by itself. I was so scattered, I didn't pay attention to what song was playing. (I wish I had because I feel that would have been a message in itself!) But as I went to turn the music off on the iPad, I noticed that the time was 11:11. That's when I knew I was not making things up. The next day, I booked an appointment to see a psychic medium to help me understand what the message was.

When I started writing this book and was getting downloads in the bath, I asked for a sign that I should start writing again and that I was in fact being guided. As I asked the question, I heard someone outside on the street scream the word *yes!* (with an exclamation point!).

I know the universe has my back. I know we are all guided when we actively choose to be present and open to receive messages, but I have been pretty slack in honouring that connection.

It's not that I don't make an effort; it's more that I spend way more time in my logical, masculine, yang, creating-and-controlling-energy mindset, rather than in my spiritual, feminine, yin, surrendering and trusting.

We all know this. Hence this Surrender Project.

It had been a while since I had asked for a sign. And I stopped seeing my elevens everywhere several years ago now.

So, I surrendered my control and sat on the beach after my morning run. I took a few deep belly breaths and connected to the universal energy. As I let my own breath sync in with the rhythm of the ocean's ebbs and flows, as the waves kissed the shore and melted away, I asked for a sign.

How do I know if I am being guided?

How do I know I am on the right path?

Call it intuition, universal guidance—or bat shit crazy.

But I heard that confident yet quiet voice come up for me again.

I have learned to trust that voice that comes from within, but I don't recognise it as my own. I heard the number thirty-three and the colour yellow or a bee.

Okay. Let's run with that.

I wanted to honour and listen to the guidance that the universe had already given me. I knew it kept giving me signs and instructions, but I hadn't been listening. It has told me numerous times to start journaling and paying attention to my dreams.

For as long as I can remember, I feel as if I have lived two separate lives because, when I sleep, I dream. My dreams are vivid, and they visit me every night. I wake up feeling as if I haven't slept or rested, but instead have run around all night visiting people. In the first hour of waking, I can recall pretty much all of it. It is usually random stuff that doesn't make much sense to me, but I guess that's the point of journaling them.

I thought this was normal and that everyone dreams. But then I started asking my husband every morning what he had dreamed about, and he told me he doesn't dream much, and if he does, he is unable to remember them.

So, I have started making more of a conscious effort to journal or pay attention to my dreams in case messages come through. But I have no idea how to make sense of them.

I did a philosophy and dream interpretation class as an elective in my psychology degree, but it all seemed pretty ridiculous and made no rational or logical sense to me. How can anyone prove that a particular dream meant one thing or another? Where is the evidence?

Says who?

Who made up these things?

Where was the link?

Where was the evidence or research to prove it?

There wasn't any, so my brain just rejected a lot of the content, which doesn't really help me now.

Last night, I dreamed that my husband slept with another woman. Am I the only one who has dreams like this? I am still trying to analyse it, but what I think I am more confused about is the fact that I wasn't even angry about it. I was encouraging it. Even awake I am still not angry.

More curious.

Am I perverted?

I know for so many of my girlfriends, the idea of their partner with someone else would propel them into a rage of jealousy. Even if it was a dream, they would wake up angry at their partners. But my dream didn't have that effect on me.

Is there something wrong with me?

On another note, I got to catch up with my best friend and her husband for brunch this week. She is heavily pregnant with her first, and it is so exciting! Something within me yearns for the same thing. I feel as if I have been ready to be a mum for over twelve months now, and I can't wait for the day when timing aligns.

It's pretty cool, though, watching most of my girlfriends go first and hearing about the journeys, experiences, and lessons they have to pass on.

As our hubbies were catching up over coffee, we went for a little walk to have some real talk, girl to girl. She has been so wrapped up in her pregnancy and enjoying her little love bubble that, to be honest, I haven't heard her complain, say anything negative about her experience, or need a good old vent for a long time. But she opened up and said one thing she has been missing is feeling sexy and being desired. She just feels fat.

We women are so lucky. We get to have that connection to our babies and experience carrying life, but I have always thought it was so unfair that we have to sacrifice our bodies and careers, rip our vaginas, put on weight, go through morning sickness, and have a little critter bite our nipples in order to bring a baby into the world. And all men have to do is enjoy an orgasm, and they get all the glory of being a parent too. Is there any way we can bring equal rights to the labour process too? I would love to see men push a baby out of their hole!

Parenthood feels like a chapter that is so close yet so far for us. I can't wait to be a mum, but I would be lying if I said I didn't have anxiety about the labour process. So far, my girlfriends who have gone before me don't have pretty, smooth-sailing stories to share. All they say is that it was all worth it.

Dan and I are celebrating our wedding anniversary this weekend, and we booked a little weekend getaway glamping. Because of the pandemic, all our travel plans were cancelled for 2020, and travel is one of my favourite ways to emotionally connect with him. It can be difficult to find time together because we each run an independent business. So I was really looking forward to a weekend away with him all to myself. I even bought some sexy lingerie for the occasion, which I was excited to surprise him with!

As I was shopping for the perfect piece, I had asked another of my best friends for some recommendations. She has always invested in and loved lingerie, and I have always loved the way she owns and honours her sexuality. But I was baffled by how much money she has spent on lingerie. I figured, what's the point? You don't wear it for long. It just ends up on the floor.

She explained it was like her Superwoman outfit. Often she wears it under her clothes for no one else to see but for her to feel. It is her power move.

I realised I hadn't taken advantage of my femininity and sexuality in a way that made me feel empowered in a long time. My work ethic was my power move, but what is the point of being women if we don't leverage our femininity? It has the power to pull tides, create life, and turn heads!

Femininity really is our superpower, but for such a long time, I had been repelled by it. I had been repelled by vulnerability, by rest, by periods, by women using their beauty to be magnetic. Instead, for years, I have been grinding trying to work, think, and feel like a man. I had been headstrong on ensuring I could do anything a man could do and never needed one, only wanted one.

I feel this worked well for the last twelve years when I was using contraception and suppressing my hormones. But for the last twelve months since I have become more aware of my natural cycle, I have realised that that way of life and work is no longer physically, energetically, emotionally, or spiritually doable let alone sustainable.

What if I did start to see my femininity as my superpower?

Some crazy things have happened since I decided I was ready and open to receive messages and guidance.

Dan and I have been wondering whether we should sell our property or hold it as an investment. When I left our apartment to go for a walk last week, I saw a lady standing at my gate staring at our apartment. I asked her if she needed help. She informed me she was just passing by. She had owned one of the apartments in our building ten years ago, and her biggest regret was selling it. She told me to make sure I held onto ours.

How weird that I had been needing guidance in deciding to sell or hold onto our apartment. How crazy that my path and the lady's path aligned at that exact time considering I really only leave my apartment once a day.

What were the chances she would be standing there at that time?

Was this coincidence or guidance?

I was in the car and thinking about how I was due for my laser treatment, but I couldn't for the life of me remember what day or what time. I randomly looked down and found my appointment card at my feet.

On another day I was driving when I decided I wanted to go for a run, but I didn't have my hat with me. Next minute, I glanced at the rear-view mirror and saw my cap on the back seat. (It's never there!)

Lots of serendipitous events like this have been happening lately. They may seem insignificant, but sometimes they are the small reminders we need that we are being supported by something bigger than us in this crazy world.

Diary Entry 20

A spiritual awakening

So, I wanted to test this spiritual connection. I've been told by a few mediums that I have the powers they have; I just don't connect with them.

The academic in me struggles to accept and explain what you cannot see or explain with research and science.

Do we all have these powers?

Is it what most people recognise as intuition but frequently drown out with noise?

This year, with my Surrender Project, I wanted to experiment and experience more of the alternative medicines. Magic mushrooms and a psychic medium were what I was being called to next.

A friend of mine recommended a reiki healer he goes to who is also a psychic medium, so I decided to suspend my expectations, trust, and be open to whatever came through. I made an appointment.

As I was walking into this lady's house, I decided to try to tune into my intuition and make a little game of seeing if I could also pick up the messages being given before she delivered them to me. I wanted to know if I was crazy and making up things in my head. Am I being self-righteous and thinking I know more than I do? Or am I actually able to connect to something bigger than I am?

As soon as I walked into her treatment room, I felt at peace and connected. It was as if my heart had been cracked wide open. I went to the bathroom first and took a few deep breaths and tried to ground into the present and pick up any energy. I don't know how to explain it, but I felt a presence. It was my nan—my mum's mum. I tried to tune in. If I was connected and trusting my intuition, what messages was I picking up?

The healer had hung flags from her window decorated with all the chakras and colours. Even though I didn't know too much about the chakras, I picked up a message that I was low on energy, and something needed to be cleared in my solar plexus as well as my heart chakra.

The healer invited me to sit in a chair, and she asked me what my intention was. What was I there for? I don't know if it's because of the sceptic in me, but my number-one rule when seeing mediums is not to give away too much because I feel as if they can then just read my body language and tell me what I want to hear. This is not the talent of a genuine medium; rather it's just good behaviour analysis.

I decided to test it out. I sat quietly and tried not to show any emotion as she closed her eyes.

She told me blue was a colour of significance to me right now. (This had also been communicated to me in my first diary entry.) She picked up that, as a little girl, I used to play with and write to fairies. She told me I needed to go back into that energetic space and believe in magic again. She said I dream a lot and my guides have been telling me to journal, but I still wasn't listening. She said I was very driven, but my focus is on logic, and I spend too much time in my head. I need to get back in my heart and surrender. She said that even during meditation—although it's an attempt for me to get back into my heart—I spend time doing and thinking as if the meditation is something I need to tick off my to-do list every day. I need to start using meditation as a time for shifting my energy and getting back into my heart.

As she opened up her book to do my numerology chart, next to it was another book *The Four Agreements: A Practical Guide to Personal Freedom (A Toltec Wisdom Book)* by DonMiguel Ruiz. Recently I have been getting signs to reread this book. I thought in my head, *Is this all woo-woo? Is this manifestation? Or are alternative therapies a real thing? Because I personally feel as if they are everywhere at the moment, and it's a way of making money by taking advantage of people who are searching for meaning in a world devoid of hope.*

I decided to conjure up a thought and put it out to the guides. I'd then wait to see if they would be messengers and pass it on to her. Could I have this conversation all in my head? Was what I was thinking being passed onto her? Or were we both picking up the same messages? It became like a game.

Within a few minutes, she spoke and said, "This isn't all hype. You get these messages too. The world is going through a spiritual awakening. People are waking up. Everyone does have these powers. We are coming into a new realm of consciousness, and more people are here to do the light work to help raise the consciousness of the collective. This isn't a fad. The reason you keep seeing these things and feeling these emotions is that we are going into an era when many people will wake up."

As she was speaking, I was reminded of using these abilities myself. But the only time I really tapped into them and used them was when I was slightly drunk, twenty years old, and travelling in Ios, Greece. I thought it was just a natural curiosity, interest, and ability I had to read people and their behaviour. (And maybe that was why I was drawn to study psychology.) But I figured it was rude to do that and judge people, so I blocked it out. Besides, what did I know? Until one night, out on a pub crawl, a guy I had met on my travels and I were playing a game and trying to read the stories of people in the bar. He figured I was pretty good at it and encouraged me to read him. I think it was partly because I didn't really know him or anyone at the bar (and I was slightly drunk), I had nothing to lose, and didn't really care what anyone thought of me, or if I offended anyone. So I just let whatever came through me come through. Don't ask me where it came from or how I knew these things, but everything from how many siblings he had, how old they were, his parents' divorce, his perception of the world, women, relationships, travel, work. It just all just vomited out of me. I had only known this guy for a couple of days (and not intimately may I add), and we had never spoken about these details before.

He was wigged out! How had I known all that (correct) information about him? And I think I was wigged out too, which is why I never again tried to tap into such downloads. It felt rude and intrusive, as if I had just invaded his thoughts, his pains, and his secrets without permission. Even though he had asked me to do it, I felt I had intruded on his privacy. We both quickly sobered up.

As the healer was reading my numerology chart, she picked up that my solar plexus and heart chakras were blocked, which confirmed the message I had downloaded when I had initially walked into the room. She put me on her table to do some reiki healing, which again made no logical sense to me, but I can't deny I felt notably lighter when she finished.

I don't know what she did, but I felt as if there was a blockage in my throat. She said she picked up a lot of heavy energy, and it was fear based. She asked if my parents had struggled with money when I was young. She felt I might be carrying around their fears. I never went without as a child, but I am aware that my relationship with money is a result of my parents' scarcity mindset around money. My relationship with money has inspired me to do what I do, and to empower women with additional income streams because I know the stress of not having enough money has on young growing families trying to do their best.

She told me to work only four hours a day in my business and to focus on just being—to ground myself and get out in nature and explore the rainforest. She said she saw me having two kids by the time I am thirty-three, one boy and one girl. She didn't see our family home coming to fruition for two years (August 2022). She described the home, and she saw it exactly the way I see it.

I left feeling lighter, but also deep in thought.

Another spiritual leader whose podcast I had been listening to mentioned that none of us are meant to walk this spiritual journey alone because we keep second guessing ourselves and thinking were crazy. So sometimes, it's good to seek help simply just to have the reassurance that we're not. There is more to life than what we can see.

I wonder how many of us have these abilities but rely on science, psychology, or drugs to justify what we intuitively know.

For a few years when I was between the ages of eighteen and twenty, I definitely abused alcohol to numb pain, but I think a lot of young adults experience that as they explore the discomfort of finding themselves and navigating puberty hormones, first love, and all the heightened emotions that come with those experiences. But I can say confidently that, for the last five years, my husband and I haven't really been drinking. I enjoy a yummy cocktail with dinner when I'm socialising, but I don't enjoy the taste of most alcohol or the feeling of being out of control. It gives me anxiety and a hangover the next day. So, naturally, when it comes to celebrations, I would rather dance all night with my girlfriends or invest in, try, or create new experiences.

My birthday was coming up and I asked a couple of my best friends and their partners if they would like to book an Airbnb in the mountains, get offline, ground in nature, and try magic mushrooms instead of a boozy night.

Magic mushrooms had been on my bucket list for a few years. We had the best crew to experience plant-based medicine. They were open to it, and with the Surrender Project, it felt like the right time.

Funnily enough, though, I was the only one who got to experience it. After a beautiful day lazing in the sun and exploring waterfalls, we mixed some magic mushrooms into honey. We set ourselves up around a campfire with blankets and tribal music under the most magical stars away from the city. I don't know what happened. Maybe I got a higher dose, or maybe I was just more sensitive to alternative states because I don't drink much alcohol or caffeine. Maybe it was my mindset going into it. But I felt it kick in nearly straight away. I lay down on the blanket as I started to float and merge with the energy around me. It was calming and connecting. The clouds started to morph into pretty pictures and talk to me as the leaves of the trees turned into metallic pink and green butterflies. Everything else just disappeared. I didn't even notice that everyone else kept talking around the campfire and even double dosed on their honey but didn't get to experience the same bliss.

It was nice. I remember thinking why would people binge on alcohol when this feeling is available too and way more inclusive and loving than adding noise, fuel, and emphasis to your existing pains and insecurities. This felt way more peaceful.

How is this level of consciousness also available? How do we miss the beauty in nature in every day? What level of awareness are we all living in? What level of awareness *could* we be living in? This made me feel as if we had been walking around blind and deaf and missing the *real* magic.

We aren't really listening or looking. Are we missing the entire point?

Diary Entry 21

Nature's medicine. And what marriage really looks like!

SINCE I STARTED THIS EXPERIMENT NEARLY A YEAR AGO, I HAVE BEEN way more in my body than in my head. And I've been more curious. Rather than running a million miles per hour, I feel as if I am floating. There is no urgency, no hustle, no force. There is a lot more space— space to breathe, space to think, and space to question.

Don't get me wrong; that little voice pops up every now and then, taunting me that I am not doing enough, working hard enough, or just "enough" in general. But I am less reluctant to buy into her shit.

Instead, I breathe and question, "What's the truth in that?"

Is that my intuition and highest self-communicating with me? Or is it just old shitty belief patterns that have been conditioned for decades that I need to let go of?

More often than not, it's been the latter.

I guess that's the thing about growth. It's uncomfortable, and we've got to be willing to sit in the discomfort to face the ugly stuff, but then also be committed and brave enough to do the work to move from there with ease and flow.

It's a never-ending journey, as I explained in a previous diary entry. We are like trees. It's our nature to continue to grow. We don't get stuck. We just stop allowing ourselves to grow because it's uncomfortable. But whether you resist it for a month, a year, or a decade, growth is inevitable. You can thrive or struggle through it. It's your choice.

Here's my latest curiosity: Do we feel good and then do good, or do we do good then feel good?

I have always understood the law of vibration (there is an entire chapter about universal laws in my previous book, *Life Above Zero*) and higher levels of energy attracting more of the abundance, but I was curious with the practicality of it as I had started to see it work in my own business.

During the weeks when I was taking the pressure off myself, letting go of expectations, getting rid of strict structure in my day, focusing more on getting into nature, and making my business fit around my joy rather than the other way around, I was personally attracting more team and clients than I had during the weeks when I was trying really hard and trying to force it.

I was still doing all the things I usually would do to build my business—adding value, writing content, speaking, podcasting, blogging, and growing my community and network—but it was coming from a place of joy and sharing my passions.

The high achiever, leader, and researcher in me was trying to understand it so I could bottle it up, teach it, and duplicate it!

But, logically, it doesn't make sense. I was doing less and achieving more.

Energetically it made sense. I was vibrating at a high frequency of joy and gratitude, and that meant people were drawn to me.

But was my energy high because I was having a successful week in business, which allowed me to feel good and take it easier? Or had I taken the pressure off and prioritised my joy and feeling good, which led me to have a successful week?

I am not sure.

I didn't say I have mastered this whole surrendering thing. My heart and head still have arguments.

My husband and I went away as we had planned to celebrate our wedding anniversary together. I was so excited to have him all to myself. Because we each run an independent million-dollar business and lead teams, our days are long. He usually gets up at 5:30 in the morning, and I don't see him again until seven in the evening. And I don't always get the best of him. I get what's left. Which is okay, as we have chosen this for the chapter of life we are currently in. Usually we travel every few months and that is our time to reconnect and invest in our relationship. But because of the pandemic, we hadn't had that sacred time together to really emotionally connect, which, as a woman (still unsure if this is a gender or personal thing), is something I crave and find myself worrying I would have to look elsewhere to find.

This is my diary entry, so I am allowed to be honest. I know I am not supposed to say this out loud, but I bet I am not the only woman who has felt like this. Craving to be seen. To be heard. To be held. To be courted. To be desired.

We had booked a glamping spot an hour away, and I was so excited to get unplugged and fall asleep to the sound of the ocean waves. I looked forward to enjoying some yummy food, a good book, and the undivided attention of my husband.

I bought sexy lingerie with the help of my girlfriend, and we had a voucher for a fancy restaurant close to where we were staying, which was perfect. It was exactly what I needed. What we needed.

I had to remind myself to never underestimate the power of nature. Just getting unplugged. Getting grounded. Sleeping under the stars and listening to the sound of the waves was what I personally needed to refuel. To calm myself. To love myself.

That's not even including the love and connection I got to relish in from my husband, connecting without distractions, making love, and then having naps in the middle of the day as you do when you're seventeen and have no responsibilities.

It made me remember the vows we had made to each other a year before in front of all our nearest and dearest at our wedding.

> I promise to always make my happiness my responsibility and work on being the best version of me and never relying on you to fill up my cup.

> I promise, no matter how full life is with work or kids, to make time for us and to invest in our relationship and stay the crazy weird one to keep the spontaneity and fun alive.

> I promise to fall in love with you over and over again and continue to reintroduce myself and get to know new parts of you as we evolve individually with time.

> I promise, no matter how mundane life might get, to make time to be grateful for each other and the small things. Because the small things really are the big things.

Oomph. If I needed a reminder twelve months in about what I had committed to, I have no idea what the next thirty years of marriage are going to be like!

My parents had just celebrated their thirty-second year of marriage. It's not until I was married myself that I understood the significance of that—what goes into making that work, staying together, still loving each other (let alone not killing each other), and not looking outside of your marriage to get your needs met.

As I sit across from my husband at this fancy restaurant, I take him all in.

His blue eyes.

His strong jaw line.

His cheeky smile.

His delicious smell.

His fashion sense (let's be honest—he dresses better than I do).

His calming nature.

This is what marriage is for me. This safe container between us. This partnership in which we support each other to explore individually and together. Life gets a little crazy sometimes, and we just need to make the time to check back in and see how your teammate is going.

Before we were married, I was really anxious about making the commitment to one person for the rest of my life. I don't know what I want next year, let alone what I'll want in thirty years. How can I promise myself to someone? How can he know he will still want me?

But what I love about what I have found with him is that it's not as if we made a promise to each other last year and everything is locked in stone and will remain unchanged for the next sixty years. We expect change.

The man across from the table from me, who has mystically grown an impressive beard recently, isn't the person he was when I married him.

F#★k! I am not even the woman I was a week ago.

I respect and care for this man.

He keeps me safe, and I'll keep him wild.

Diary Entry 22

Periods. Yep. I said it and I am going there

THE SURRENDER PROJECT HAD BEEN ENCOURAGING ME TO LEAN MORE into my feminine and explore the female cyclical nature. My girlfriend Chan is a moon goddess, and over the years, she has passed on her wisdom to me. But you know what they say—you can't help someone unless she wants to be helped.

This year, although I had known about this "surrender" stuff, I was hearing it differently. I was ready to learn, to trust, to rest, to admit I didn't know it all, and that what I had been doing was no longer working. I wanted help feeling more connected and guided.

I had been tracking the moon a little bit more closely, and I had also been tracking my period to understand my fertility window. Dan and I had decided we wanted to start trying for kids sometime in the next twelve months. I felt as if I had unlocked my superpower. Also, at the same time, I felt a little cheated.

I find it ironic that, up until I was twenty-seven years old, my period was an inconvenience. It was annoying. It was dirty. It was embarrassing. It was gross. It was taboo.

Now, however, as I embark on my thirties and I'm surrounded by friends who are trying to conceive, I see it as a gift—a gift I had taken for granted. So many of my friends did not have regular cycles because their hormones were suppressed after decades of contraception. We were not educated about this, and we didn't celebrate and support our beautiful, innate feminine wisdom.

I am not sure if that is a message that is consciously or unconsciously communicated to young women who are growing up, but it's definitely the one I got through society and advertisements telling me I could still play sports, swim, and wear that white dress confidently and be the life of the party if I used those glossy-packaged sanitary products.

Ignore your period. Skip it with the pill. Or even better get rid of it all together with the rod. It's no big deal. It's not powerful. It is just a nuisance that gets in the way of everyday life.

I was learning that, historically, bleeding has been recognised by tribes and many communities as a sacred time for women when they are encouraged to relax, recharge, connect to their intuition and dreams, and lean on other women for emotional support. But in the Western world, despite the fact that our hormones dictate that we need that sort of attitude, we are told to continue to work, think, and live like a man and push through it even though we are energetically drained and our emotions are out of alignment.

No wonder so many of my girlfriends were burning out and suffering from adrenal fatigue and hormonal conditions, polycystic ovaries, and endometriosis. And they were spending tens of thousands of dollars going through in vitro fertilisation (IVF).

I can't help but wonder if the situation would be different if we, as young men and women, were taught about the beautiful gift of the menstrual cycle? What if it was celebrated and honoured? What if we recognized and respected the wisdom it brings when we understand its effect on mood, energy, libido, and fertility throughout a woman's month.

Would men and women understand each other better because they would realise we are wired differently? We are not just shitty versions of each other?

Would more women and men be empowered with contraception, understanding a woman can fall pregnant only on certain days, rather than believing that sex is bad and women need to put fake hormones into their bodies to avoid unwanted pregnancies? What if they realised that the contraceptives could cause lifelong damage that could surface when a woman wants to bring new life into the world?

Would more women feel empowered and at peace knowing that there are certain days when she is energetically wired to get more done and others when she is required to rest. Wouldn't this be better than feeling as if she is broken, not enough, and not measuring up, berating herself for not feeling like Beyonce every single day?

I'm not being sexist or making excuses for women. This is science. Women have a twenty-eight-day hormone cycle whilst men have a twenty-four hour one. Magnetic resonance imaging (MRI) scans have also found that male and female cognitive pathways are different. Women's brains are more functionally interconnected, engaging both left and right hemispheres, which helps with multitasking, intuition, and emotions, whilst men's brains cause them to be more focused and unilateral, meaning they are better just focusing on one thing and are less influenced by emotions.

We are wired differently. Energetically and intellectually.

Men aren't just hairy women doing it wrong and not paying attention, and women aren't just emotional men who overcomplicate things. Our biological differences need to be understood and respected if we are to have harmonious relationships so we can complement each other.

Since tracking my period and the moon, I have felt so much more connected to myself and Mother Nature. I am not just a ball of emotions. I am not a crazy, emotional bitch. Quite the opposite actually. My mood, my energy and my sex drive are predictable. My feminine and masculine are both needed. And now they are honoured.

I will admit that, up until I began this Surrender Project, I was pushing myself and held myself to the same standard an ambitious man might hold himself to. Yet I wondered why I didn't feel as productive, energised, or on purpose as the men seemed to be even though I matched (even exceeded) their effort and work ethic.

Now, since tracking my cycle and the moon, I feel nurtured. I know how to look after myself as a goddess (and the boss bitch I am).

I now know I am all four seasons. I honour the season I am in, and I know it will pass.

The week before I bleed is my autumn. I am sensitive. I experience anxiety more often and start to feel energetically drained and start to crave hibernation. I become more reflective and like to write and journal rather than speak and coach. I enjoy massages, cleaning out, and cleansing spaces.

The week I am bleeding is my winter. I am introverted. I need more self-love and affection from my husband. I enjoy warm cacao. I rest. I enjoy baths, movies, and cuddles. I meditate and feel more intuitive than normal.

The week after I bleed is my spring. I feel creative and inspired. I love to speak, create, move, and listen to music. But I also tend to become overwhelmed quickly because I go from zero to a hundred quickly and take on lots of projects with my newfound energy.

The week I am ovulating is my summer. I feel sexy and mischievous. I want to do my make-up and hair. I want to have fun and not work. I want to get dressed up and go out dancing with my girlfriends. I want sex. I start to notice other men. (It's the wild woman in all of us who wants to mate!) I want to socialise. I want to be seen. I want to be wanted. I am magnetic, flirty, and social. I can also be selfish, reckless, and not as thoughtful as I usually would be.

Here's a fun fact: Studies have found that researchers can predict when a woman is ovulating (is most fertile) if they look at a series of photos of the woman taken every day for a month. Turns out that we unconsciously start to wear less clothing the closer we get to our fertile time. It's as if we know innately when we are "ready." It's the way we lure in a male to mate.

Since I have surrendered to and honoured my feminine nature, I feel more empowered and magnetic, and I get more done with flow instead of force. I now understand the importance of both the yang (doing) and yin (being) energy and no longer berate myself.

But I am also disheartened when I think of the millions of women in the Western world who have only been told one side of the story. Our power as women isn't found in go-go-going. We have superpowers that men don't have. We are intuitive. We are emotional. And we are dynamic.

We get more done by resting. (And let's be honest, when we are "doing" we can double men's output because our brains allow us to multi-task whilst theirs struggles to.)

The moon pulls tides all around the world. We humans are 70 per cent water. The academic in me has started to realise and understand that the moon affects us too.

After tracking the moon and my cycle, I now know what days to have sex to bring life into the world. What a powerful decision, and now I can be in control of it. I have only recently started to seriously contemplate this magical yet scary concept.

But that's a diary entry for another day.

Diary Entry 23

The "now"

THIS YEAR I PUT ASIDE A LOT OF MY USUAL PERSONAL DEVELOPMENT, investment, and business books and focused instead on spirituality books and courses to learn more about different levels of consciousness and this fad word *manifestation*.

I was contemplating what it means to have "now" because, at the end of the day, that's all we really ever have—the now.

But what level of consciousness do you need to be in to experience the now?

So many people say that a level of presence is needed to experience joy. But the devil's advocate in me can't help but think of Holocaust survivors sharing their stories of trauma and torture. Being in the now was definitely not their place for experiencing joy or happiness. Life was deeper and more complicated than that. A lot of them realised that, despite being tortured and physically abused, if they could be somewhere different in their heads, they could be in control of their freedom. Nobody could take that inner peace away from them.

Freedom is the separation of your body or form from attachment. It's not necessarily the now in physical form. It's being. It's the expansion that's hidden behind the thoughts.

If you just give presence to what's in front of you, as if you are an observer, life moves through you, and you don't need to achieve or want something. This makes life separate from you.

The present moment is the field on which the game of life happens. When you've made peace with the present moment, life plays the game through you.

I am a realist, a researcher, and an academic. As you know, I'm also a recovering human doing. But I still maintain that life and business go through seasons of strategic imbalance.

But, if you spend two years absolutely miserable just to be "successful," you've missed the point. I have been learning through the Surrender Project (and my life in general) that we are meant to enjoy each of those now moments because that's all we have.

Yes, things aren't always going to be fun or pleasant, but we've got two options:

1. Accept it (whatever it is) rather than carrying around an emotionally charged narrative about it that doesn't help anyone or make you feel good
2. Enjoy or be enthusiastic about it

That's really it.

The now can be as magical as your wedding day or as mundane as folding up the washing. It's still all we have. You may as well choose to be present and have your consciousness floating around taking it all in and capturing lots of mental happy snaps (or the not-so-happy ones that no one sees, like the explosive poo nappy!).

But it is your unique experience. It's your scrapbook of mental sticky notes that remind you of all the beautiful human experiences you got to witness in your short time here on earth.

Whether you believe your life experiences are guided, predetermined, written in your stars, or just sheer luck, it's still all you've got, and all you will ever have.

So why not start seeing the wonder in it?

Presence is consciousness without thought. Without judgement or attachment.

It's freedom.

It's peace.

Spiritual teacher Eckhart Tolle explained this so beautifully in his book *A New Earth*, which I read as I was starting to ponder the same things. He explained that, when we want to arrive at our goals more than we want to be doing what we're doing, we become stressed. The balance between enjoyment and structural tension is lost, and the tension has won.

When there is stress, it is usually a sign that the ego has returned, and we are cutting ourselves off from the creative power of the universe. Instead, there is only the force and strain of the ego wanting, and so we have to struggle and "work hard" to make it.

Stress always diminishes both the quality and effectiveness of what we do under its influence. There is a strong link between stress and negative emotion, such as anxiety and anger, and this stress is becoming recognised as one of the main causes of degenerative diseases such as cancer and heart disease.

Unlike stress, enthusiasm has a high-energy frequency and so resonates with the creative power of the universe. This is why Ralph Waldo Emerson said, "Nothing great has ever been achieved without enthusiasm."

Upon reflection, I realised that a state of joy and enthusiasm is most commonly my natural state. People recognise me and are drawn to me for my energy, my outlook, my perspective. I don't think anyone has ever sat down and actually taught me this theory or how to implement it when I was younger. I think I just worked out at a young age: when I feel good, I do good.

And sitting in feelings of unworthiness, guilt, failure, resentment, blame, shame, or justification doesn't make me feel better or inspire me to come up with any solutions. It doesn't help me be the wife, daughter, student, friend, or sister I want to be, so I don't see the point in holding myself prisoner there.

When I catch myself experiencing those emotions or in those states even now, I feel them, but I quickly take action to change my state. Because it doesn't feel good there. It doesn't help me or anyone around me, so why spend more time there than I need to?

I am just wasting my now.

But I look around at people I work with—my coaching clients, women I work with in business, and even friends and family members with whom I have heart to hearts. So many still haven't worked this out yet and are giving their peace away—their now—because of their egos. Their suffering is self-imposed. They don't realise that, yes, pain in life is inevitable. But suffering is a choice.

Once again, I want to quote Eckhart Tolle because he explains this so much more eloquently than I could and he doesn't offend as I might with my directness. He explains some of the most common "excuses" people use—reasons why they give their now away:

> There is something that needs to happen in my life before I can be at peace (happy fulfilled, etc). And I resent that it hasn't happened yet. Maybe my resentment will finally make it happen.

Something happened in the past that should not have happened, and I resent that. If that hadn't happened, I would be at peace now.

Something is happening now that should not be happening and is preventing me from being at peace now.[7]

Often the unconscious beliefs are directed towards a person so that "happening" becomes "doing":

You should do this or that so that I can be at peace. And I resent that you haven't done it yet. Maybe my resentment will make you do it.

Something you (or I) did, said, or failed to do in the past is preventing me from being at peace now.

What you are doing or failing to do now is preventing me from being at peace.[8]

All these statements are assumptions—unexamined thoughts that are confused with reality. They are stories the ego creates to convince us that we cannot be at peace now or cannot be fully ourselves now.

Being at peace and being who we are (being ourselves) are the same thing. The ego says, "Maybe at some point in the future, I can be at peace—when this, that, or the other happens, or I obtain this or become that." Or it says, "I can never be at peace because of something that happened in the past."

So many people's stories could be labelled "Why I cannot be at peace now."

---

[7] Eckhart Tolle, A New Earth (Australia: Penguin Books, 2018).

[8]

The ego doesn't know that our only opportunity for being at peace *is now.*

With the Surrender Project, I was starting to realise, as I leaned into my spirituality (as well as over the years trying to find answers externally, whether it be in coaching, courses or programs), that we don't always get what we want, but we always get what we need.

So often I wasn't finding the answers externally, which obviously wasn't what I wanted (or paid for), but it was what I needed to remind me that all the answers are within.

I understand mentorship because mentors can quicken people's journeys by teaching something they have already learned. But I am curious: if people stopped investing thousands of dollars in coaches, programs, and courses, and instead had the discipline to sit in silence for thirty minutes a day, meditate and journal, would they find all the answers they were looking for? For sure, they would save a lot of money, but I think they would also be richer in gratitude, joy, and inner peace.

We all have this intuition, or guidance from our spirit team. I have been learning how to consciously tap into it, and we can all do the same, but so often, we just drown out the connection. Eventually, I learned that I was just paying thousands of dollars every year for other people to confirm what I already knew deep down.

Sitting in silence, leaning into my intuition, and journaling was so much nicer than filling my head with all the noise, the contradicting opinions, and advice of other people who thought they were experts on my life and knew what was best for me. Self-reflection in any form was cheaper (who doesn't love free stuff!) and so much more empowering than berating myself, telling myself I suck, I am not enough, I am not doing enough, I don't know what to do.

Because that is false. I do know what to do. We all do.

We just doubt what we can't see, but on some unconscious level, we intuitively know.

Take a breath. Give yourself permission to be here in the now. Happy in the now. You don't need a reason to be; you don't need to justify why you deserve to be. It's your birth right and your natural state.

Enjoy it.

Diary Entry 24

Work ethic doesn't equal worthiness

THIS SURRENDER PROJECT HAS BEEN A REALLY GOOD OPPORTUNITY TO not only slow down, but to check in with myself regularly. As a coach, I've got so good at calling other people out on their bullshit, and it's been nice to reflect and have a good look in the mirror and clean up my own backyard.

Every year on my birthday, I reflect on the biggest lesson I've learned over the last twelve months. As I sit and ponder this on this birthday, I notice that I still have a feeling of guilt about slowing down. Something unconsciously tells me that the only way to be successful is to keep working hard, the way I had for the first few years in my business.

I used to take pride in the fact that I have a great work ethic, and that has brought all my success. Nothing has been handed to me. I worked hard to create it for myself, by myself.

I hit a massive professional goal and pinnacle leadership position within my company during my birthday week this year. It was ironic because, as I was becoming recognised, I was getting a lot of beautiful messages celebrating me: "I don't know anyone more deserving,"

"You're a unicorn, Lauren!" "I don't know anyone that works as hard as you. You've got such a great work ethic."

These kind messages were confirmation that others saw me the way I did. But they also made me feel guilty because I realised I don't work hard anymore. It is as if people deserve respect for working hard to achieve success. Work ethic is like a yardstick we use to measure our respect for ourselves and others.

Am I still deserving of my success?

These comments also made me realise that "hustling" isn't cool anymore. For most people it feels unattainable and not something people aspire to do (including myself). A few years ago, working ourselves as hard as physically possible was glorified, yet over the last two years, I have realised it's just not sustainable. This especially applies for women as we aren't wired the same as men—we are cyclical. And besides, now, being in flow is the new cool.

I'm all for flow! But I do think it means that, in the process of making it cool, we've now also vilified hustling. It's no longer sexy to hustle. I've noticed within my business it can be really polarising to have an energetic work ethic because a lot of people say they can't do what I do, or they just don't want to do what I do.

It's as if *hustle* has become a dirty word, and women are no longer inspired by hustling, working hard, or maintaining a high-energy work ethic. Comments like this trigger me because I genuinely don't think we have to work hard to be deserving of our success.

But, because I am a straight shooter, I value transparency, and I am so over people buying into social media's highlight reel—you can trust me to tell you the truth and not just what people want to hear that is going to make them feel comfortable.

So, trust me when I say that those people who are enjoying flow spent at least one season hustling.

To achieve anything or get anything off the ground, we need commitment and energy. Reaching a goal takes a burst of inspired action, and we might have a bit of strategic imbalance for a while as we create what we want, but it won't stay that way forever.

Although I threw a lot of energy into my business at the start, and my job was tough in the early days, it was only tough because I was building up an income around a full-time job. If I didn't have the work ethic to get started and continue to show up even when I didn't feel like it (let's be honest, most days it would have been easier to sit on the couch after a ten-hour day at my job), I never would have gotten anywhere, let alone where I am now.

It didn't stay that way, though, because I was in flow and I loved what I was doing. I persisted, I mastered the skills I needed to grow my business, and as my confidence grew, so did my income. I simply believe that we must have a passion and put in the hard yards to set ourselves up, and the rest will follow naturally.

The last two years of my work haven't been "hard." Yes, I've been consistent. I've been passionate. I've been committed to my growth and stepping out of my comfort zone, taking inspired action, and having uncomfortable conversations (those things come hand in hand with leadership).

But I have also had good boundaries, I've scheduled my joy every day and have made sure I've prioritised my own health and happiness. I don't believe that these strategies take away from my success at all. My income continues to grow, and I keep creating more white space, new opportunities, and freedom.

So, if this guilt over slowing down wasn't coming from the idea that I had to swap time for money (because that's why I chose the network marketing profession—it provides residual income), where did it come from?

People who come from wealthy families rarely stop to consider if they are worthy of that abundance. They were born into it, so they don't doubt that they're deserving; they just accept that is the way things are.

The flip side is that, when working-class people like me come into money or start creating money that they don't necessarily have to work hard for, they start feeling they have created a dishonest way of life. It's almost as if they think they are cheating the system or doing something wrong because they're not working hard to create their wealth despite the fact they have seen so many of their loved ones working hard their whole lives.

This realisation has been my biggest breakthrough as I work through the Surrender Project because guilt about achieving abundance while slowing down has been my biggest blockage.

I obviously do believe that work ethic equals worthiness, and I guess that, in this project, I have been trying to understand it so I could flip it since it was no longer serving me.

Because when I dig deeper, I do know that we can create more and do less, business can be easy, wealth can come easily, and none of those things makes you less deserving of abundance.

Real talk, though: I still do honestly believe that, to get anything off the ground, in order to create flow and build abundance, we do have to expend an energetic work ethic or hustle at the start to get momentum. Of course, we then need the skills and confidence to maintain the momentum.

My highest value is time freedom and flexibility. So, I worked hard for a season, which was only around three to five hours each day on top of my full-time job to get my business off the ground and build that residual income stream.

But I only worked hard so that I didn't have to continue to work at that level, pace, or intensity forever. I want to spend my time with my husband, my friends and family members, and my future kids. I want to enjoy being a stay-at-home mum, relaxing at the beach, prioritising my own health and happiness, and spending more time researching, reading, and writing.

What is hard work anyway?

Maintaining our efforts and committing to being consistent to get a side hustle or business off the ground whilst juggling a job is hard. But is it any easier doing nothing and staying in a job that requires you commute two hours a day; miss magical moments; receive a capped income; and also feel unfulfilled, uninspired, and hungry for more?

There is a big difference between working hard and hard work. Yes, I worked hard for a season to set myself up and get momentum in my business and build my brand, but it wasn't hard work.

If you align yourself with your highest values and passions and work out a way to either monetise them or create a lifestyle so you can enjoy them, you want to show up and put the work in. Because it's important to you.

The currencies of life:

1. Money
2. Audience or your relationships (your network)
3. Time

I believe we need to leverage at least two of these currencies to create the third one.

For example, you leverage your time and audience to create money (either by selling a service or product).

You leverage your audience and money (by outsourcing, hiring employees, or paying for systems to automate) to create time.

You leverage your money and time (by investing in your network) to create more audience and to be connected or introduced to other high achievers or world thought leaders, influencers, and business owners.

When I first started, I didn't have the money, but I had the time, so I focused on building and investing in my relationships with content and value to create the money. And now I use my money and audience to create the time I was missing.

It's not dishonest to make money easily—it's smart!

157

There are so many ways to create wealth these days that no longer require us to trade our time or work hard for it.

I know beliefs are just thoughts we keep thinking. They are tools to help us get where we want to go. When we're experiencing frustration in any area of our lives, it usually means there is an old belief system that needs to be updated, and when we're being triggered in any area of our lives, it usually means someone or something has contradicted one of our beliefs.

So here we are. My beliefs have helped me get here, but they aren't helping me go where I want to go next.

So, I am committing to:

- Continuing to look for evidence to prove that money, success, and business can be easy.
- Writing and reading my new affirmation daily. Let it be easy. My business and wealth continue to grow with ease while I focus on joy!
- I will stop asking people what they do for work when getting to know them. Instead, I'll ask them what they do for fun, what they want to consciously create this year, what they dream about, what are they passionate about.

Likewise, when people ask me what I do, I will respond with, "Do you mean with my time or for money?" Because my work and work ethic have nothing to do with my worthiness. I am worthy of love, abundance, success, and time (we all are). We don't need to do something or be someone impressive to deserve it.

Likewise, we don't get medals at the end of life for suffering, crawling, struggling, burning out, or being martyrs, so instead I plan on dancing around the sun for as many more years as I am gifted with, loving life and looking after myself with zero guilt!

Diary Entry 25

What it means to be a woman in the twenty-first century

I AM NOT ENDING THIS YEAR AS THE SAME PERSON I WAS WHEN IT started. I feel I have totally upgraded the software my computer (aka mindset) has been running on. This year, and through this Surrender Project, I have delved deeply into my beliefs and the conditions I held around money, work, and marriage.

And I am so glad I did.

This contemplation bought me time and a calm space (without the judgement or ego) so I could make sense of who I am, what I stand for, and what I want. Without that opportunity to get clarity, I wonder if I would have blown it all up and missed out on this chapter of life where I have never been so in love, so supported, so grateful, and so blessed with abundance in relationships, purpose, health, and wealth.

It's not until we give ourselves the time to slow down and really sit with our thoughts and the space and the commitment to unpack them that we realise that our personal worlds are reflections of our thoughts because they stem from our beliefs, and our beliefs trigger the emotions we feel.

And that's your world, right?

It's not objective. It's subjective to our perspective, which can be manipulated by the way we choose to look at it.

So, if we can change our beliefs, we can change our thoughts, which changes our emotions, which changes our experiences and our reality.

I was so ready to unlock a new reality. The beliefs I have held to this point (about money, work, and marriage in particular) had served me and got me here, but they had me feeling restricted when all I wanted to do was to expand, with ease, flow, and grace.

During the Surrender Project, I have realised that all I needed to do was let go of my beliefs and allow myself to think bigger, give myself permission to receive more, be more flexible, be softer, lean into my feminine, and trust the flow rather than trying to control it.

As I worked through this project, I wondered what had inspired me to build such strong beliefs and conditions around working hard for money, having pride in my work ethic, being independent rather than owned by a man or having my desires suppressed or constrained by marriage.

I realised that a big part of it was the role feminism (or what value I personally perceived feminism to have) in my generation.

Our generation of young, empowered women was unique. We are unlike the generation of our mothers and grandmothers who went before us. We have more opportunity, we have more rights, we have more to prove, we also have more to lose, and we have more to do. We have more wisdom passed down from the generations before us, as well as their pain, their uncapped potential, and unrealised dreams (because they were restrained and restricted by the patriarchy).

We now have the opportunity to realise our own dreams, do and have it all, and not rely on a man or allow a man the power to take it from us.

Unconsciously through this project, I realised that, not only had I internalised that and felt that obligation, privilege, fire, and hunger deep in my soul, but I also felt the weight and experienced the contradiction in it.

The women before us have worked so hard to fight for women's rights to work, to earn, to vote, to be heard, to lead, and to live just like men. But, in our feminine nature, we innately crave to nurture. We can have it all; in fact, my generation of empowered women have felt the need to prove it can be. But I personally feel that our success is due to an awareness that our mothers didn't have the luxury of having it all, so we don't want to abuse that privilege. It's a struggle that women in our generation uniquely face as we try to literally grow humans, look after families and homes, and build careers, all the while keeping up with our male counterparts because we should feel grateful that we can.

But we are burning out. We are giving up. Our adrenals are through the roof. Our fertility and femininity are being lost and becoming something we need to learn to harness rather than just feeling it as something of our nature, essence, and being.

Women in our generation are expected to work like men, but we are still wired as women. We are cyclical. The traditional work force isn't built to cater for us. It's not that we are broken; we are just sick of trying to fit into a mould that wasn't built to allow us to fit in it in the first place. That is why more and more women are starting their own businesses, freelancing, and joining the network marketing profession.

This need to make the most of the opportunity I was gifted with as a woman in the twenty-first century as well as the obligation I felt I owed to the women who came before me who didn't receive that gift not only affected my beliefs and thoughts around my work, career, and wealth but consequently influenced my resistance to being controlled or owned by men in relationships and marriage, which in turn influenced my thoughts, feelings, behaviour, and then my reality.

I would never let a man feel that I needed him. Neither would I allow myself to be in a position in which I actually would.

I would never let a man see me as weaker than he, which meant I would match him in work ethic, effort, strength, output, masculinity, resilience, income, and education.

But the more and more I tried to live and work like a man, the more I felt like I was being robbed of the gift of being a woman. Of being soft. Of being protected and looked after. Of being and honouring my cycle instead of constantly doing. Of being allowed to slow down to enjoy being just a mum without also feeling the need to have a drive to create and have success outside of the home.

I started to see how this was playing out in my marriage. I started to see my husband as a teammate rather than my king and someone I had to keep up with rather than someone I would allow myself to lean on. And sexual chemistry (no matter whether you identify as straight, bisexual, or gay) is always the attraction and strategic dance between a feminine and masculine energy. He was playing his role, but I wasn't playing mine, so instead I started doubting monogamy. I wondered what it would be like to crave and look for that domination or desire outside of my marriage.

But what I have come to realise within this experiment is that, if I just allow myself to sink more into my femininity, that power dynamic is available in my marriage right now. But I was showing up as a male not only in my business, but in my marriage too

I know I have been like this for the last decade. Hunger and obligation have driven me since I was eighteen to create what I have and to protect myself from getting hurt. So, my husband married me for these reasons knowing who I am. But I also wondered how our marriage would evolve and expand if I were to soften more and allow him to be my king.

Could I also give him that gift of being his queen?

I started to delve into more books to help support me in relearning my nature as a feminine energy in a relationship. How do I show up and support my husband so he can be the king I am craving? I know he wants to be; the problem is that I don't allow anyone to fill that role. This goes along with the fact that I don't like not being in control. I don't like being looked after and having to rely or trust that someone will show up and support me when I could just rely on myself and support myself without enduring liability or vulnerability.

The books that helped me shift the most have been *Do Less: A Revolutionary Approach to Time and Energy Management for Ambitious Women* by Kate Northrup and *Keys to the Kingdom*, a novel by Alison Armstrong. I am not going to lie; as I read both books, I initially cringed. They triggered me. But I know that's because they were contradicting my beliefs that were so deeply rooted around the concepts of working hard, being independent, and not having to soften around a man. But I also knew my beliefs were no longer serving me, so I was open to changing them in order to change my experience.

I've been hard, masculine, doing, achieving, challenging, and it had served me for a season, but if I persisted any longer, I knew I would burn out. It was as if my feminine was screaming to slow down, to be soft. To allow myself to be looked after. To not feel guilty for prioritising my body and home in preparation for a family and to allow my man to go work without the guilt that I can no longer keep up with his stamina.

Is this just a cycle of what it means to be a woman?

Maybe I needed the Surrender Project to help me break down all my limiting beliefs, relinquish control, and allow my business to grow while I do less—without the guilt—in preparation for motherhood?

Was that what this year and the Surrender Project were preparing me for? Motherhood?

Diary Entry 26

Are you sure you're ready?

It had been a while since I went to a psychic or medium. I was feeling a little lost and as if I wasn't working towards anything. Actually, it was more than that. Despite my efforts, I was not seeing any real shifts or changes externally in my life.

Like magic, the same week I had been thinking about making an appointment in hope of receiving some reassurance or guidance, a woman called Susan from the United States, who was completely unknown to me, reached out on Instagram and asked if she could do a reading for me.

You would think I would know better by now (especially after immersing myself in the Surrender Project), but I struggled to have faith and believe in what I could not see. So I kind of cheated on faith and played a little game. I had been seeing dragonflies everywhere lately. Big ones were somehow finding their way into our bedroom despite the fact that we kept our doors and windows shut. I had come to believe these creatures were little universal signs or guides letting us know that I was on the right path and to keep trusting.

So, as crazy as I sounded to myself, I said out loud to my spirit guides before my reading, "Make this psychic mention the dragonflies so I know this connection is real and I'm not crazy and making it up."

During the reading, Susan spent forty minutes telling me a lot of things I wanted to hear—things I had personally and privately been hoping for, and things that only my husband and I knew about. So I was excited yet also sceptical thinking that surely life doesn't get to be this good. When does it happen? A part of me just didn't believe her—until the very last two minutes when she said, "Oh, by the way, your spirit guides wanted me to tell you that, although you connect with birds and butterflies, dragonflies are your sign."

Ooomph!

And just like that, my ego got slapped in the face, my walls came down, and I fell straight into my feminine, trusting, believing, and knowing that I was (as we all are) supported by something bigger than all of us.

I have the word *faith* tattooed on my wrist. Also, the same word, in cut-out wooden letters, hangs above our bed. I don't really understand it yet, but faith has always meant something to me even as a young child (and not in the religious sense). It's as if it's already been written in my stars, and my purpose in this lifetime is to understand my relationship with it. Funnily enough, that week my husband and I were violently awakened when the letter *F* fell off the wall in the middle of the night, just missing conking us on our heads! I had a little chuckle to myself. Yes, I know. I hadn't been listening and having faith, so it needed to literally knock me on the head to remind me and get my attention!

I continued to honour my feminine energy, needing some extra loving. I could feel I was more fragile than normal this week, and this project had helped me get better at listening to her when she needed nurturing. So I booked myself in with an energy healer who (also mysteriously) had reached out to me the same week and asked if she could do a clearing on me.

As I felt her running her hands over my body, I could feel some kind of communication and exchange of energy transmitting. It was as if she was hearing my most vulnerable secrets, and I wasn't speaking a word. This felt so different to my initial experience with a kinesiologist. My body and my soul were open to it. I needed it. At the end of the healing, we sat on the couch, and she relayed what she had picked up from my body and my spirit guides.

We both cried. She could feel my heaviness. My heart. She told me that I still wasn't listening. I wasn't resting. I wasn't slowing down. And I was burning out.

She asked if babies were on the cards soon. Little did she know Dan and I had been open to receiving for a few months, but nothing had been happening. My faith had started to dwindle.

She said she felt a baby's energy hovering around me, but she wasn't sure if I was really ready yet. She asked me if I felt ready for what having a baby would mean for my life, my work, my business, my expectations (both of myself and others), and my fast pace.

I thought I was.

I had just come off a *big* weekend with all my team who had travelled to the Gold Coast for a business event. Being an introvert, energetically I felt drained, which I had expected. I knew I would need some time to myself to retreat and go inwards.

But, also, being an empath, I had taken *all* their energies on—the weight of their dreams, their goals, their wishes, their pains, their fears. I felt it all as if it were my own. In return, I felt obligated to give them all of me—my heart, my presence, my love, my energy, my wisdom, my lessons, my time, my promises that I would do everything I could to help them be happy and get where they wanted to go.

But I was learning I just can't be everything to everyone.

That is where this release was coming from.

I want to care for you. I want to be there for you. But energetically, I can't do that for everyone. So, on the back end of it, I beat myself up because I want to give so much but I feel that I'm not doing enough, caring enough, helping enough, being enough, loving enough.

I knew it.

I had heard it a hundred times before. F#*k! I had even preached it myself and written a book about it! But it finally started to integrate: looking after yourself isn't selfish! Having boundaries and saying no to others isn't selfish. Empowering others to help themselves and taking yourself out of the equation isn't selfish.

If I can't love and look after myself, I am no help to anyone.

That is the season of life and business I am in.

Up until now, I have felt as if I have had to keep striving and pushing myself. And it's not even for me anymore or to prove a point. For this point in my life, I had worked hard (and smart) and was exactly where I wanted to be. I did it to prove to other women that they can have beautiful careers, health, wealth, and abundance. I kept showing up and doing the work because I wanted to be the example, cheering women on, letting them know they can do that too! And if I take a step back, if I were to really honour this season of rest, I would feel guilty for not leading and being right there next to them supporting them.

But as the Surrender Project was teaching me, we all go through seasons, and I needed to start accepting and honouring that this is my season.

It's a season of rest and consolidation.

Yes, women can *have* it all and *be* it all, but we actually don't have to. In the pursuit of trying to do that, we are also denying our femininity. It's okay to receive. It's okay to slow down. There is empowerment in that too.

Obviously, I am still navigating that myself, and it feels foreign to me.

I drove home from the healer's house with questions in my mind: Am I really ready for a baby? Am I meant to be a mum? I am the healthiest and fittest I have ever been. I have just completed the 75 Hard Challenge. Am I really ready to hand my body over to someone else to use as their vessel?

I decided I was going to listen—really listen—to what the psychic and reiki healer had told me this week. I know it wasn't new. And another kinesiologist and psychic had given me the same advice six months prior, but I was now ready to listen.

This new chapter is all about me slowing down and being selfish. More self-worth and energetic boundaries. No more gym, strict routines, or expectations. I would allow myself to sleep in and prioritise meditation and yoga. I would really implement what I was learning from the books I was reading on femininity too and spend more time in my body—dancing and listening to music, getting massages, and being sensual and looking after myself. Because, when I am happy, my husband is happy.

In my marriage, I would allow Dan the space to talk; I wouldn't fill the space between words or try to solve his problems. I would be a safe space for him. I would allow him the opportunity to please me and surprise me without having to control and organise everything because he wants to look after me. And when I allow him to, our intimacy and my sex drive increase. I feel like the queen of the kingdom, powerful yet soft in my femininity.

It was finally starting to click. It had taken me a while to integrate what I had spent the last twelve months learning and writing on these pages, but I felt things shifting.

Diary Entry 27

Motherhood

I HAVEN'T WRITTEN IN MONTHS, SO WHAT'S UP?

I let go.

I stopped documenting and analysing my thoughts and just committed to living life, day to day with no goals other than just being present and enjoying it.

Previously, surrendering used to make me feel like a fraud, not actively pursuing and hustling towards certain goals. But I had confused acceptance with acquiescence. I worried that peace would lead to stagnation.

But I have realised that things are earned with "work." But work is not the same as suffering. Work is just work—sending out emails for campaigns, creating content, hopping on coaching calls, and mentoring my team. But worrying about output, results, engagement, and sign-ups is suffering. Why would we believe the suffering has anything to do with the success we manifest?

We can enjoy what we do and take inspired action every day without ruminating and being attached to the outcome. It is still progressing and moving forward. Just without the suffering.

So that is what I have been doing—finding the joy in each day no matter how mundane it may be, trusting the process, and surrendering to the outcome.

Then …

I fell pregnant.

Actually, as I write this, I am thirty-two weeks pregnant. And now the last two years make total sense. Isn't hindsight a beautiful thing!

This Surrender Project came to me when it did because there was so much I needed to learn and live to prepare me for this journey.

As I reread my previous entries, I can't help but laugh at how naive I was to think this project—the emotions, the challenges—weren't on purpose. To think I was lost or not being guided.

I was exactly where I needed to be. I learned what I needed to learn—to become the woman I was destined to become.

It is all evolution.

It was all in divine timing.

But that's the thing. We don't know it when we're in it unless we have faith.

We must trust and surrender.

And, oh my gosh, has that been what the last thirty-two weeks have been for me!

For the first time in my life, I am *not* thriving! I have just been surviving one day at a time. I am totally embarrassed for the lack of empathy I have previously had for other pregnant women who are part of my life, both professionally and personally. I never knew or was able to conceptualise just how much growing a human can literally take everything from you—your identity, your energy, your drive, your discipline, your health.

This pregnancy broke me.

This pregnancy also made me.

I know pregnancy affects every woman differently, and I don't know if some women are just lucky, forget the first trimester, or just handle it like a freaking superhero. But, initially, pregnancy broke my spirit.

The initial excitement was quickly invaded by the nausea. And the nausea and vomiting was relentless.

I spent most days from week eight to week twenty-two crying. I wanted it to stop. It was like waking up and reliving a severe hangover day after day. Whoever called it morning sickness lied! It lasts all freaking day!

I've felt the heavy waves of guilt—guilt knowing I wanted this and received it. I should be so grateful! This is the biggest gift. I had prayed for this, and so many women will never have the blessing of carrying a baby. I felt guilty that I was not working and was spending most of my day on the couch or in bed hugging a spew bucket. I felt guilty that Dan was working all day then having to come home to a house that looked like a bomb had hit—half-eaten random pieces of food on the kitchen bench, and dog poo on the balcony because the smell of everything was so intense I couldn't clean it up. I felt guilty that, after a long day, he was still the one who had to organise dinner and do the housework. (Which, let's be honest, for about three months was just picking up Mexican takeaway and hot chips on the way home because that was all I could stomach!) I felt guilty that I wasn't able to show up and support my team the way I had previously been doing for the last six years, and I didn't want them to doubt how much I cared. I felt guilty that I wasn't nourishing my baby and body with healthy foods when they needed it most. I felt guilty that I wasn't showing up as the woman I had secretly promised and hoped I would be stepping into this next chapter of life.

Pregnancy is not what I had expected or envisioned.

Then the waves of doubt crept in.

I would often think, *If I can't even get through the first trimester, how the hell am I going to get through the rest of it?* When people talk about the challenges of motherhood, my fear has always been around the birth or the lack of sleep and all the things that come once the baby is earth side. Not once had I thought this part would be the hard part.

If no other women were talking about this part of motherhood, were the challenges of pregnancy just relative to what was still in front of me? If that's the case, I don't know if I can do this.

Then the fear would engulf me.

I am such a big believer in the mindset, and I was so worried about what my negativity was doing to my pregnancy and my baby. Could I wish this away?

But no matter what I tried, I couldn't will myself out of this feeling. I would end right back where I started.

Surrendering.

During the days I spent snuggled up on the couch, I found myself bingeing on a Netflix series called *Sex/Life*, and I instantly recognised myself in the main character—the feelings I was experiencing; the doubt I had at the start of the Surrender Project; craving more passion, sex, novelty, and spontaneity. Doubting monogamy and marriage.

I felt the pull—which I have now learnt to trust—to start writing again. I heard the quiet reassurance and confirmation that women need to read about the Surrender Project. Women need to hear the crazy inner workings of another woman's mind in the twenty-first century to know they are not alone, and the way they are were feeling in society's social constructs of marriage, motherhood, and the workforce are normal.

The Netflix series *Sex/Life* was a massive hit. It seems every woman online was addicted and raving about it whilst men thought it was rubbish. This affirmed to me that it was speaking directly to women's psychology, addressing what women today think, crave, and desire yet suppress and are too scared to talk about or admit out loud. But viewers could live vicariously through the main character in the series.

Women are continuing to evolve. We are no longer fitting into society's social constructs that have been created for us, predominantly historically by men.

We want more (or different) options in the workforce. We want more (or different) options in the bedroom and in marriage. And we want to create wealth and impact life in a way that nurtures our feminine being rather than damaging it.

We are slowly breaking out from society's expectations and cookie-cutter moulds that have us feeling restricted, contained, and unfulfilled. We are learning to surrender to and come back to our roots and innate women's wisdom. It just takes a few of us to go first, challenge the status quo, and be brave enough to speak out loud what most of us are thinking but are told we are crazy to ask for.

I needed this Surrender Project. The more I talk to girlfriends and women I work with and mentor online, the more I realise other women need it too. We are not alone in our desires or beliefs.

As I write this on the other side of the first trimester (actually enjoying the last few weeks of my final third), hindsight has once again blessed me with an understanding of my journey and the gifts in my challenges.

Having a rough pregnancy has definitely erased my fear of childbirth. It has instilled in me the self-belief and confidence that, if I can survive that, I can survive anything!

Women really are warriors.

But without the Surrender Project, I would have struggled even more with my self-limiting beliefs about work, money, and marriage. I needed to be okay with slowing down, with accepting help, with leaning on my husband, and with working less.

I am not lying when I say I got hit with every complication under the sun with this pregnancy. Every challenge was just preparing me for the resilience and faith I needed for the next.

I think this pregnancy has tested me more than anything in my entire life. This baby girl (yes, we found out!) is going to be one wise little cookie if this is how much she can teach me from the womb.

The last six months, despite my best efforts to be productive, to be resilient, to be strong, to be stoic, to be solution focused, this little lady has manifested something pretty much weekly that sits me right back on my ass—legitimately. And I have had to not just talk about surrendering; I have had to embody it.

Every time I said I was listening, she knew better and hit me with another whammy or complication.

I've been quiet and not writing because I've been looking after me and bub and just taking it day by day, which is never how I have lived before. I've always been running a million miles per hour, but this project has prepared me to slow down and be kind to myself, reminding me the power of rest, femininity, and faith.

What seemed like two years of internal work with no progress externally was the epitome of what we can manifest when we have faith, relinquish control, and surrender.

The psychic medium, the energy healer, my spirit guides, and ultimately my own intuition were right when they said that all I needed to do was have faith and trust the process, find joy in the work, and be detached about the outcome or suffering in anticipation of it.

Time caught up.

We moved into a beautiful home that is pretty much identical to what I had on my vision board. I found a bucket list diary entry in which a twenty-four-year-old me described how I envisioned and wanted my life to look and feel like five years from then. I am now exactly where she had always hoped I would be for this chapter of life—physically, mentally, spiritually, professionally, and financially. I am in love with life, my husband, and career. I am healthy and a few weeks away from giving birth to our baby. I have always been excited to become a mother.

My husband has been my king. I have leaned on him and needed him—a lot. He has leaned on me too, and I have been able to support him through my femininity and softness. We have never been closer or more in love. And I have never been more attracted to him. There is no one I would rather do life with. He really is my soulmate (and I have never believed in that), but I honestly don't believe anyone could be better fitted to my soul's desires, needs, or wants.

He is my person.

Lucky, we didn't sell our apartment twelve months ago when we were thinking about it and our spirit guide sent that lady to my front gate to advise us not to. Twelve months later, we sold it for nearly double what it would have brought back then!

My business is having the biggest months ever even though I am personally having the slowest and most beautiful quiet months loving and looking after myself whilst my independent inspired leaders are creating lives and careers that align with their highest values, desires, and feminine superpowers too!

I feel safe and secure. I am basking in the gift of enjoying slowing down as I wait for our baby to arrive whilst also allowing my business, income, and impact to continue to expand. This is why I said yes to this profession. This is why I led by example for so long—for this exact chapter.

I am so blessed to be feeling so expansive in a chapter of life in which most women have been forced by social constructs to restrict and contract. I cannot take my blessings for granted. So many women have to make sacrifices when they become mothers going from two incomes to one. Many feel unsure as they are most often the ones who personally have to surrender their income, financial independence, and their identity in the workforce, along with their security and savings as they embark on becoming a mum, which I believe is probably when they need it most.

I get to order this *and* that off life's juicy menu.

This is why I chose this business and the network marketing profession, although I don't think I could have ever anticipated just how much I would need and appreciate being surrounded by such a beautiful community and sisterhood. Something magical happens when you surround women with support and mentorship and introduce them to a vehicle that enables them to work in a way that honours our feminine and cyclical nature and enables us to create leveraged income. It's how we used to live and work back in the days of tribes—leaning on each other, sharing the workload, collaborating, and benefitting from elders passing down feminine wisdom and empowering young women through life's different rites of passage.

Women are not meant to navigate life alone or independently, and there are just some things men can't provide us and will never be able to understand (no matter how lovingly they try).

Now, to enjoy the last few weeks of my pregnancy, share my love with my husband before we multiply and two become three, and I bring my own woman into this crazy world.

Diary Entry 28

The metamorphosis

I STARTED THIS SURRENDER PROJECT AT THE BEGINNING OF A WORLD pandemic. I was twenty-seven years old navigating the transition from maiden to mother and also unravelling parts of myself and beliefs that no longer served me but also got me where I had always wanted to be, full of abundance, free, empowered, passionate, in love, and the owner of a successful international, multiple-seven-figure business.

But I felt energetically blocked and as if I was no longer moving. It probably didn't help that the government physically wouldn't allow anyone to move either with two years of lockdowns, restrictions, and mandates!

I write this now at age twenty-nine. I am thirty-four weeks pregnant and waiting for our little cherub to arrive.

I read my previous pages with so much compassion for the girl I have been and how much I have grown. Although I know she is part of me, I don't recognise her anymore. The woman who writes this last chapter has gone through a metamorphosis:

- She is softer yet more powerful.

- She is more patient.
- She isn't driven by checklists or achievements.
- She has given up her time lines and instead has a deep inner knowing.
- She listens to and trusts her intuition.
- She isn't influenced by what everyone else is doing or what she thinks she's "supposed" to be doing.
- She no longer finds her worth in her work ethic; rather, she finds it in her being.
- She has stopped worrying about letting others down and instead makes sure she protects her boundaries and doesn't let herself down.
- She's okay with saying no and not giving a hundred per cent of herself to everyone all the time.
- She's okay with not being the bubbly, happy, positive energy that people need; instead, she allows people to sit in their own discomfort and find that energy within themselves.
- She accepts help and has stopped trying to control everything.
- She listens more.
- She works in seasons.
- She's more grounded and flexible.
- She has stopped trying to save everyone and instead believes in their ability to save themselves.
- She no longer experiences anxiety when doing nothing and slowing down.

Two years ago, I knew something had to change, so I started writing, reflecting, resting, and unpacking and discarding limiting beliefs that no longer served me. I thought it was because I was burning out and what I had been doing was no longer working as I felt I was constantly met with resistance.

But now I know that it was preparing me for you and motherhood.

I'm so ready.

My team members and my mentors have seen this transformation before their eyes over the last two years. The Surrender Project is not just a book of diary entries written on a page. It has engendered not only a mental shift but a metaphysical one.

It's evident in my posture, my leadership, and my boundaries. I have never felt so calm and supported. Who knew surrendering could be so powerful?

As I close the last chapter of this book and look forward to starting a new phase in my life, I reflect on what the Surrender Project has taught me. I am honoured to pass it along to you:

- Never underestimate the power of music and nature. To ground you, to drown out the noise, whisper your truth and connect you to something so much bigger than you.
- Your heart knows things your head can't understand. She can be trusted too.
- When you can't work it out, feel it out.
- Stop paying for shrinks, coaches, healers, and psychics to tell you what you already know. (This will save you a lot of time and money!) Sit down in silence and write. You already have within you everything you need. You have the answers; you just need to have faith and trust in yourself to act on them.
- Joy-inducing activities are money-making activities. Follow your excitement. It's your third star.
- If I were to follow you around, would I know what your dreams and values are without you telling me? Your daily actions manifest the life you say you want even if you can't see it yet. That life or something better is coming if you continue to show up too.

- If you need to profess what you want, you still aren't embodying it.
- When people say you work hard, really it's your resilience they are admiring. It is your ability to throw everything at it and trust and to continue to show up and do the work when you can't see the results yet. So, it's not hard work they are in awe of; it's your faith in something you intuitively know but you can't see yet. It's what you have that others are missing.

Baby girl, I can't wait to meet you. I was made to be your mum. I am so excited to pass on the wisdom in these pages (I am sure you're here to teach me a-lot as well).

Respect your femininity. It's your superpower.

And, here is some advice for my future son (my spirit guides tell me you're in my stars too): trust your intuition, It's not just a feminine superpower; you can tap into it too. Although your real superpower is being a gentleman, romance and chivalry are not dead. These don't make you soft; they are your biggest flex. Be a king and you'll attract a queen. Together you can build empires and grow and enjoy life together. In a world that demands that women be as strong as you, let her be strong but nurture her softness behind closed doors. Be her retreat.

And this is an invitation to you, gorgeous woman, reading this: Surrender. It's the most beautiful, uncomfortable, and soul-enriching project you will ever embark on. I can't wait to hear all about it!

Lauren x

Printed in Great Britain
by Amazon

21413907R00116